Tiny Songs

Haiku & Meditations

By Terry Hermsen

With Artist Cadine Navarro

Bottom Dog Press
Harmony Series

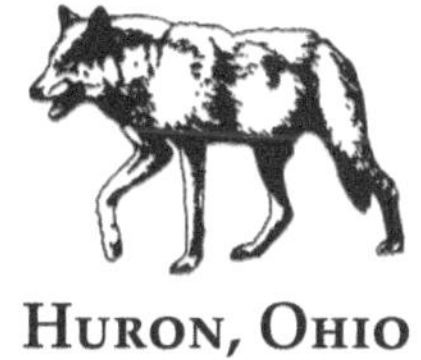

Huron, Ohio

ISBN: 978-1-947504-43-1
Bottom Dog Press, Inc.
PO Box 425, Huron, OH 44839
Lsmithdog@aol.com
http://smithdocs.net

Credits:
General Editor: Larry Smith
Cover & Layout Design: Susanna Sharp-Schwacke
Cover Photography: ©Bill Walker
The cover is of nine native Ohio prairie seeds: Milkweed, Switchgrass, Wild Bergamot, Butterfly Weed, Echinacea, Black-Eyed Susan, Dogbane, Little Bluestem and Big Bluestem.
Seed Sound Artwork: ©Cadine Navarro, *It Sounds Like Love*

Permissions

Permissions for these poems was granted from the following publishers and executors:

- Carolyn Forché, "Song Coming Toward Us" from *Gathering the Tribes* ©1976. Permission of the author via the Clegg Agency.
- Li-Young Lee, "Build by Flying" from *Book of My Nights.* ©2001 by Li-Young Lee. Reprinted with the permission of The Permissions Company, LLC on behalf of BOA Editions, Ltd., boaeditions.org.
- Susan Mitchell, "Blackbirds" from *The Water Inside the Water*. ©1983 by Susan Mitchell. Used by permission of HarperCollins Publishers.
- Charles Simic, "Stone" from *Selected Early Poems*. ©1999 by Charles Simic. Reprinted with the permission of George Braziller, Inc. (New York), www.georgebraziller.com. All rights reserved.
- David Wagoner, "The Death and Resurrection of the Birds" by David Wagoner, was granted by Robin Seyfried, his widow and literary executor.

This book of tiny songs takes us on multiple journeys.

First of all, a journey to the seeds of a new language, like an inverted cup going from the surface down to the seed, and then back to the surface to flourish. This level reminds me of Gabriela Mistral in "Poema de Chile" (1967), where the prairie babbles a new language to tell a new and more just country, where the "wild and dusky knowledge" that Hermsen traces in children's early speech and in the sound of seeds begins reaching beyond the bounds of language.

It's also a mystical journey. Mistral called Neruda a "matter mystic," and I think she would not disagree if I call Hermsen an "earth mystic." Each part of this book entails a part of a mystical journey. Here, after experiencing Cadine Navarro's artwork, Hermsen slowly comes to believe again that art might have a role to play in our times. A little light to keep burning.

Finally, it is a journey into memory. In highly evocative and poetic prose, *Tiny Songs* takes the reader from a bedroom to multiple parts of the world. From Western Europe, to the western U.S., the slopes of Canada, the Arctic, Brazil, Japan, Hermsen goes further collecting images of despair and chaos, hope and revelation.

The Chilean poet Raúl Zurita says we would not have poetry if we had been happy. Hermsen is definitely more optimistic. Even in danger, in pain, he recovered the capacity and the happiness of singing, knowing the size of a song in front of a terrible world.

In his poem to Big Bluestem, he asks us:

I wonder if you will sing with me now
no matter where my eyes are

Read this book and I promise you will listen to these seeds. And you will end up singing.

—Christian Formoso, Universidad de Magallanes
Punta Arenas, Chile; March, 2024

Other Books by Terry Hermsen:

From Bottom Dog Press:

36 Spokes: The Bicycle Poems (1985).
Child Aloft in Ohio Theatre (1995).
O Taste and See: Food Poems (2003).
Edited with David Garrison
The River's Daughter (2009).
A House for Last Year's Summer (2017).

From NCTE (National Council of Teachers of English):

Teaching Writing from a Writer's Point of View (1998)
Edited with Robert Fox.
Poetry of Place: Helping Students Write Their Worlds (2009).

Table of Contents

Dedication

In homage to the hidden strands of the earth.

So we are left with a stark choice: allow climate disruption to change everything about our world, or change pretty much everything...to avoid that fate. But we need to be clear: because of our decades of collective denial, no gradual, incremental options are now available to us.

—Naomi Klein,
This Changes Everything (2014)

Love's the only engine of survival.

—Leonard Cohen, "The Future"

Introduction

Welcome to *Tiny Songs.* In an age where so much of the viable life on earth is threatened and where the powers that be, whether governmental or corporate, media-bound or educational, religious or cultural seem so entrenched in clinging to control, like many people I have had a hard time knowing how to respond. What would a poem or a song, an essay or a teaching lesson—all that I've spent some 50 years of my life engaged with—have to offer?

And so, after reading Naomi Klein book, *This Changes Everything,* where she calls for radical moves to face the truly radical challenges ahead, I tried my best to do just that, *change everything.* For instance, I mostly stopped writing poems, and poured that energy into climate action, reaching out to others in the area for ways to respond. Quite consciously, we started working locally, having learned from people like Rob Hopkins of the Transition Town movement, Helena Norberg-Hodge and her emphasis on shaping local economies, and Daniel Wahl with his call for bioregional regeneration, for paying close attention to where we are and building on its strengths.

Progress has been slow. But in getting to know who's here, who cares, who's willing to put in long hours, who might collaborate with whom, we've begun to form the basis for long-term action. Right now, we're working on changing how we live upon the land, looking to shift the monoculture of the suburban lawns that surround us toward a gradual array of prairies, wetlands, forests, rivers and wildlife corridors. In the face of resurgent fossil fuel dominance and increasing carbon emissions, this all may seem rather small, but it's what we have to offer. And from this, we may find ways to foster significant land-based change from this our part of the planet.

It's a tiny song, in the midst of a whirlwind.

I see the pieces of art in this book as tiny songs too. As small ways to ground myself—like the prairie seeds in Cadine Navarro's artwork—in what has been here for thousands and indeed millions of years, the life-forms that preceded us, and on which we still so deeply rely, and for whose flourishing so many people around the globe are working to restore.

After experiencing Navarro's seed-sound-produced images, I began to believe again that art might have an important role to play. As I will explain in more detail later, she found a way to capture sounds made by native prairie seeds, mostly below our hearing, and bring those sounds to our awareness through her art, which became the floor of the museum, instead of being hung on the walls. I was part of a team bringing audiences to see her art. Over those months, for some reason I began writing haiku, that ancient Japanese art which I have always deeply treasured. Almost unconsciously, I kept a part of my days awake, usually at dawn or when heading to sleep, to small songs that I could record quickly and then hone over the course of a week or so. Along with those poems, I tried my hand at miniature essays, or meditations, to help me reflect on what her art seemed to be saying to so many visitors, including myself. Like so many participants in her exhibition, I found my central perceptions shaken to the core.

Then one day, near the closing of the show, I spent eight hours by myself in that space with the seeds. Listening to their quiet sounds, sleeping at times beside their images, the museum doors closed, the light still glowing from the floor. The third section of this book reflects the spontaneous writings that came from those hours, paying homage to each seed, one by one. Written at the edge of consciousness, as if I were not me but a correspondent in their world, I present them not so much as refined pieces of art, but as an attempt to tap down into that primordial soup of sound and awareness.

* * *

I offer, then, this book as a brief call—something to dip into while we do the rest of our work as we speak and act and gather in the service of what the earth most needs now, a transformation of consciousness and behavior in this time of challenge and renewed, necessary hope.

Part One: Tiny Songs*

Nocturnes
Cold Spring
Summering
Autumnal

*Special thanks to Christian Formoso for assisting in the translation of some of these poems into Spanish.

Nocturnes

This winter's moon
somehow trapped below
the ledges of the ice

In far off mornings
my lips often find themselves
speaking with you

Late winter wind
tell me how long your heart
has been scraped this raw

I once knew a child
who'd rather been born a river
and lived inside me

Astilla de luna en mi
ventana—como un recuerdo
la memoria crece

Sliver of moon
in my window—as a memory
memory grows

Tarot reader
places her table just beyond
the museum doors

Old woman searching
for words—lifts her hand
and pats the air

How many times
has this worry stone
gone through the wash

Sleeplessnight—
he hasn't quite figured out
where his arms go

Waking—hands enfolded—
last night's moon still passing
through the clouds

This thread runs through
tiny eyes—then back up
toward heaven

Threadbare bellows—
leather cracked through—
makes for a pale fire

What tune is the tick
of my little wind-up clock
trying to begin?

That's me over there
she says—peering across
the crowded lot

Winter night—he cracks open
the fifth floor window
of the practice room

Puckered blushing face
of the oboist seems to be always
on the verge of laughter

How far off my tongue moves
in a mouth rounded
by migrant vowels

This coat rack—my hat
above—seems at times
more me than me

Bebé que ries detrás de mi—
aprendiendo tu lengua—
llévame allí

Baby laughing behind me—
learning your language—
take me there

Dream Haiku (i)

Returning the musicians' car—
seats and instruments
already stolen

Falling alarm clock—
caught by my temporarily
gracious pillow

Forget speech—
learn the brisk language
of vagrant winds

Future one—must I
remember everything
for you?

¿Futuro debo
recordar todo
para ti?

Before you, there was your name
wandering my tongue
as beautiful rain

Cold Spring

Don't fear, little bird—
the nest you cling to
is lined with feathers

Moon and magnolia—
how long you have traded
your pearls and slivers of light

How many trees
will we meet if go on
embracing them this way?

Midnight under the apple tree—
the moon tries on
some whispering slippers

Even with your face
in the midnight doorway
I long for your face

Unpacking the house
of the dead—we bring with us
their empty hangers

He stands on a stage
and talks of planting seedlings
while the forests burn

Reaches for his dark-
rimmed glasses, picks up his
dark-rimmed scissors instead

(America)

By noon, morning calls
of owls long replaced
by the ricochet of guns

City moon—no stars—
and yet we expect you
to keep on singing

Dream Haiku (ii)

Calling at midnight—
crickets whirr—only the full moon
held to my ear

Llamando de noche—
zumbido de grillos—sosteniendo
la luna en mi oido

Is that at last sleep—
the tangled place inside
where our shadows meet?

Niagara at night—
weight of the water swallows
the cameras

Five currents in one river—
did you see them too—and also
tell no one?

Used to just drink
from this eternal spring—today
I drench my head

End of the concert—
old man hauling out the trash
lingers at the microphone

I wake up weeping—
all night along the prairie
they were handing out dreams

Enemy house—gone
dark now—still shines
in my mind's eye

Ah—forgiveness—
half-moon floating at the bottom
of the pool

All day writing—in small
script—about our time
in that distant town

¿Ambos despiertos–
en nuestras tierras lejanas
nos levantamos juntos?

Both sleepless
in our disparate landscapes—
why not wake up together?

How, dear moon, did you
manage at last to bury yourself
in these trees?

Two figures clinging
along the forest path—maybe wishing
they could become trees

Lake Hope—so far
the only thing I know
is your name

Crossing the bridge—
quiet reservoir below—
remember to close your eyes

SUMMERING

Solstice sky—
are kisses allowed
in the last hour of light?

Pathways through the prairie—
we play hide and seek
with glimmer

Waterfall, cliffside—
which of you has the other
most memorized?

Early June morning—
even the wrens arrive
with dreams of you

Early June morning—
amongst my neighbors
one open window

(house riddle)

No door and yet
there's entrance—pause for a brief
pool of afternoon

Solstice sky—
fireflies gather above
the burdock

Solstice sky—
she balances the wine glass
between her toes

More moon haiku—yikes!
Blame it, this round,
on the opening sky

Goldfinch trembles
bent coneflower stems
one by one

¿Ah granjeros—qué han
hecho—volviendo verdes
sus campos con petróleo?

Ah farmers—what have you
done—turned your fields
green with petroleum?

Early rising moon—
come to bicker again
with the wheatfield

Birthday balloons—
always floating to the highest
rooms of the house

Globos de cumpleaños—
flotando hacia los altos
cuartos de la casa

Good thing about death,
Zita says—at least you don't
have to pack

Foolish me—
using the wine
to scrub down the table

Yes moon—she's gone—
you might as well
wake me

Summer comes with floods
now—canoeing the streets
of Montpelier

Scrape up boreal forest
the size of England—who the hell
made you Saruman?

How to fly out
from a broiling cauldron?
Europa, these are my tears

Ice cream truck driver—
must be tiring—all day
with one song

Silent meal together
blanket—sky—stirring
sigh—taste

Dream haiku (iii)

Cardboard you—in the waterfall—
real you laughing far off
across the water

Forgive me, Love—
the haiku keep coming—each day
on this earth is yours

Behind trees—children
laughing on their trampoline
vanish into language

This night's heightened moon
waits till the fireworks
are over

Autumnal

Dry pair of milkweed pods—
how elegant now
that your seeds have flown

Little boat of moon—
don't worry—these clouds are only
the edge of the hurricane

September, forgive me
I'm trying to weigh
the heart of this fire

Street fair closing—
they walk hand-in-hand
what remains

Street fair closing—
the musicians wander off,
whispering now

So many days without you—
the trees are already
reversing their stories

Equinox, city—
streams of high clouds passing
from glass to glass

Fields of the Equinox—
the sheep, already golden,
turn away toward light

Dream haiku (iv)

All these years weaving—
on your loom—such hiding
spaces for children

To sleep, Orange-ji—
and whisper your candle out
The saints are coming

See how your carver, Orange-ji
bends so gently
to kiss your forehead

Half-moon, why here—
five planets arrayed in your slim
necklace of loneliness

Sin tu voz, amiga—
la música de la noche
ha rogado para sueños

Without your voice, friend,
the music of the evening
goes begging for dreams

Clambering up the ravine
piled high with leaves—
reach me your bright hand

Qué extraño—
comer de nuevo
del plato de los muertos

So very strange—
eating once more from
these plates of the dead

Clearing the garden—
dead tendrils cling madly
to the trellis, love

My dear November—
did you mean to leave
my heart without a name?

Made a mistake—
tomorrow's the night
when sea moon laughed with us

Fold the back of one hand
gently into the palm of the other,
making me and you

Fallow orange moon, you too—
the other half of your heart
darkened?

Turn this too, my dears,
around—light as rotation,
pregnant as sound

Tonight you give me
endless dreams—but none
of them have verbs

Tender solstice—
stretching out from home—wrap
your shadow around me

Solticio de ternura
extendiéndose desde casa—
envuélveme con tu sombra

Earth-light burial—
may my bones brighten the prairie
softly from below

Part Two: Meditations on Cadine Navaro's *It Sounds Like Love*

In 2019, artist Cadine Navarro had an idea. After 10 years of working with human voices to capture the nature of sound, she switched directions and began seeking out new sources...this time with the sound of *prairie seeds.* Collaborating with Janice Glowski, *It Sounds Like Love* exhibition Curator and Director of The Frank Museum of Art at Otterbein University in Westerville, Ohio, she proposed the project of recording the sounds of nine native Ohio prairie seeds in their dry, dormant state. In a sound-reduction space, they placed a highly-sensitive microphone—custom-designed and built by UK sound artist Jez Riley French—on groups of those nine seeds, finding (much to everyone's surprise) that even without the seeds growing or sprouting, tiny sounds or vibrations appeared! She then used a process known as *suminagashi,* which she had learned from one of the last living masters in Japan, to "translate" those sounds into the images you see in this book. Whereas in traditional suminagashi, wind or the passage of a hand makes images appear within circles of ink on water, here the sounds from the seeds—played from below—moved the ink on the water into these patterns. Not stopping there, Navarro and Glowski had those images laser-etched onto large panels of glass, which were then placed into the floor of the museum, creating an alluring visual—and quite physical—space where the main source of light came from below our feet and the sounds of the seeds which produced the artwork played from speakers around the room.

The effects of her exhibition astounded us all, for it was like no other piece of art we had experienced. It felt like entering a quiet but engaging chapel, or a transformed meditation space. Or as if a curtain had opened into an experiment in evolution at its ancient core, touching our consciousness in ways few of us had expected, awakening us in very physical and visual ways to the dynamic realities of the earth that daily surround us without our knowledge. Visitor after visitor became immersed in these seed-images, not as pieces of abstract art but more as statements from the living world itself. The expansive panels take what is tiny and give it a larger voice to shape our experience, reversing roles of the normal human vision of our own importance. By taking in what the seeds have to say, I hope in these short meditations to reflect on art's role in bringing us through our current climate emergency and helping us reach toward ways of being more directly connected with our companions on the earth.

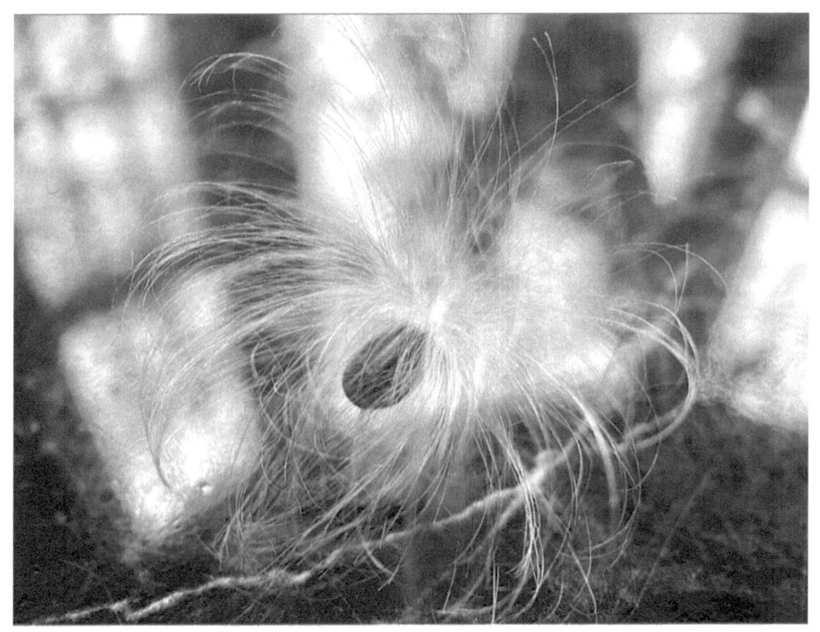

Photo: Courtesy ©Bill Walker

Photographs From *It Sounds Like Love*
Cadine Navarro (August 2021 – September 2022)
The Frank Museum of Art
Otterbein University
Westerville, Ohio

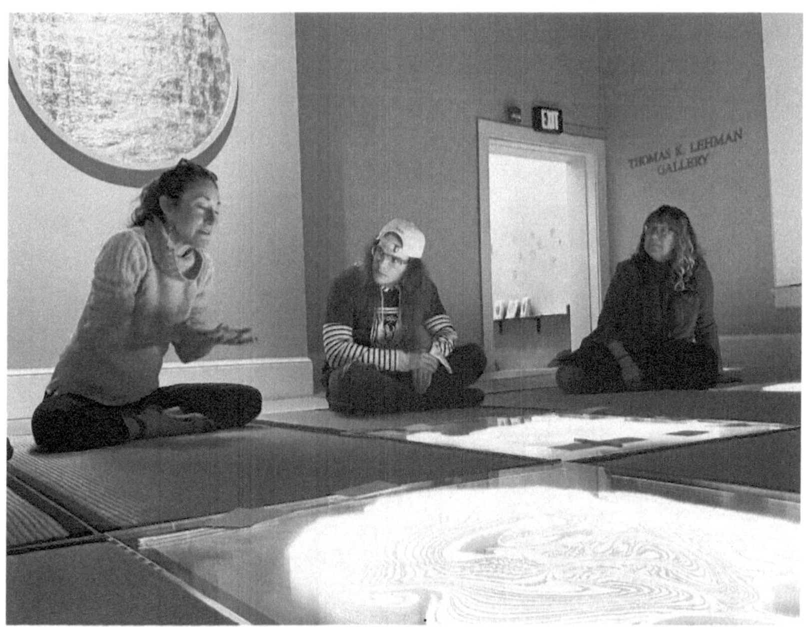

Cadine Navarro, left, meets with a class from Ohio Wesleyan University. Above her is one of her "Gold Seed Bank" pieces, with native prairie seeds covered over with 24 karat gold leaf. These can be planted, with the seeds sprouting through the gold.

Photo: Courtesy ©Bill Walker

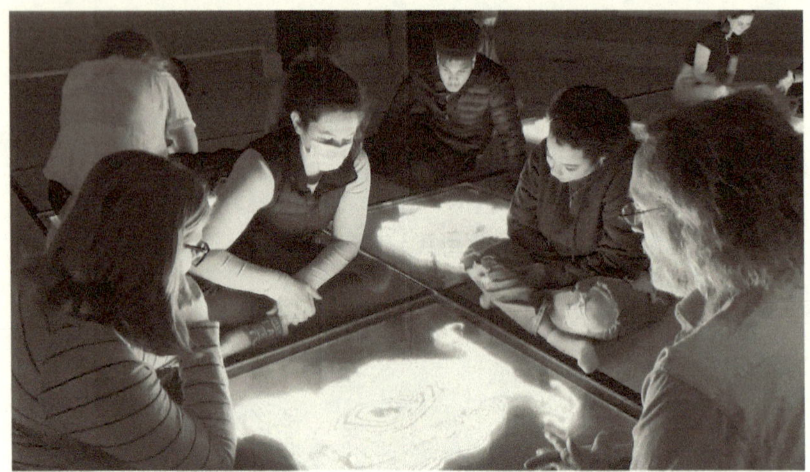

Terry Hermsen, right, discusses Echinacea with students from Otterbein University.

Photo: Courtesy ©Bill Walker

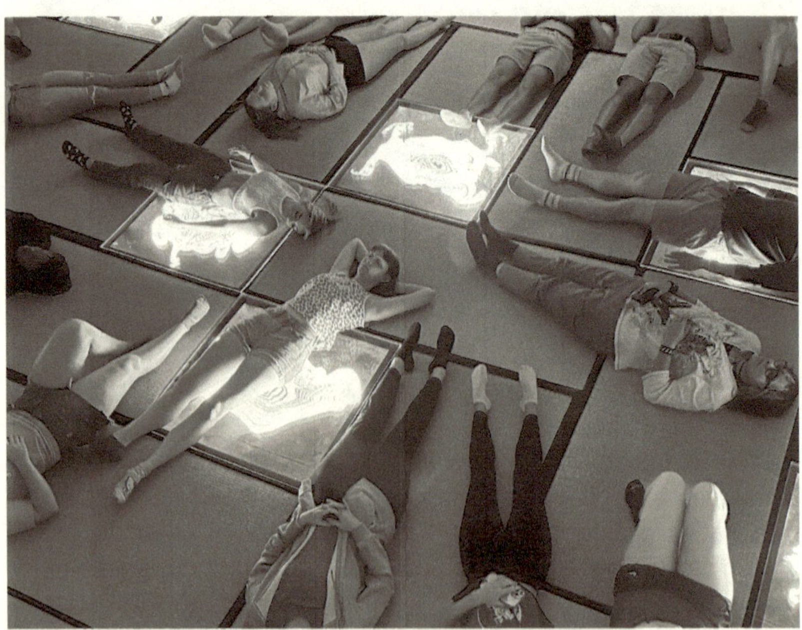

Students from Ohio State University participate in a meditation exercise conducted by Janice Glowski, laying on the art, which is indeed the floor itself.

Photo: Courtesy ©Cadine Navarro

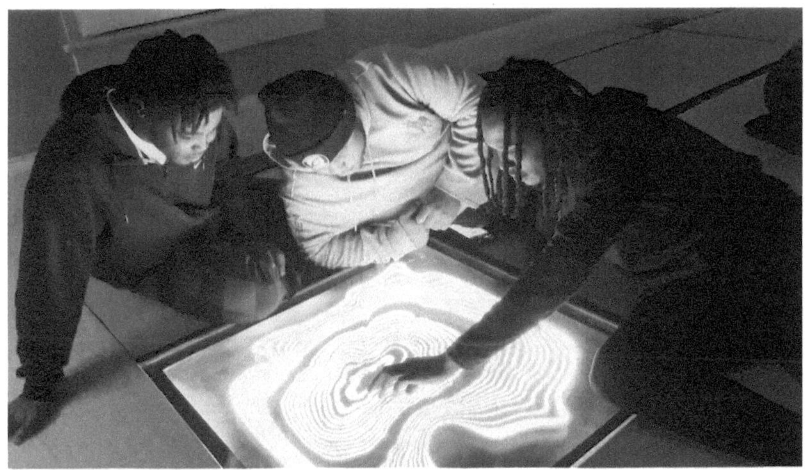

A student from Otterbein University explains what he sees in the center of Dogbane.

Photo: Courtesy ©Bill Walker

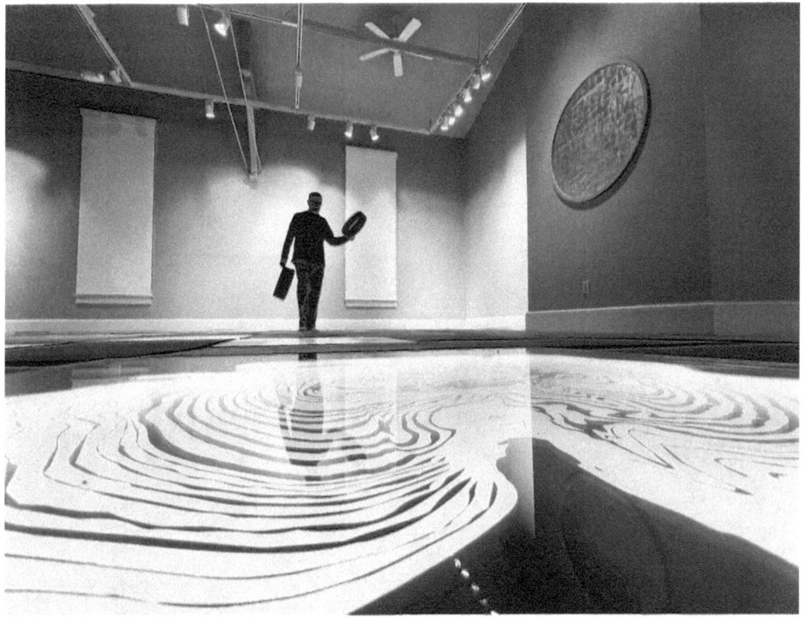

Musician Bill Walker seems to be crossing the waves of the art.

Photo: Courtesy ©Sophie Ansel

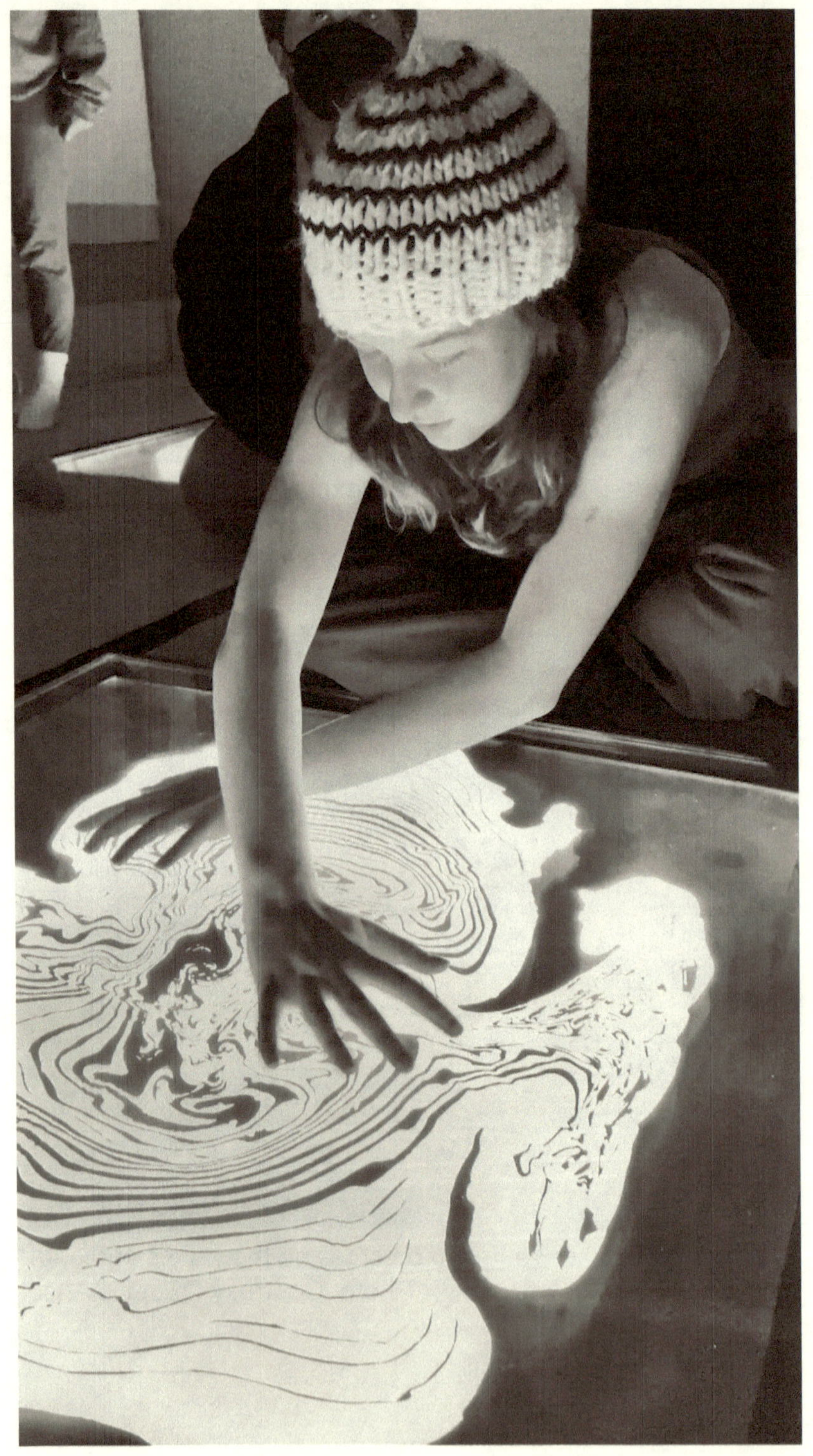

Left: A student from Otterbein University traces out her sense of an “explosion” inside Black-Eyed Susan.

Photo: Courtesy ©Bill Walker

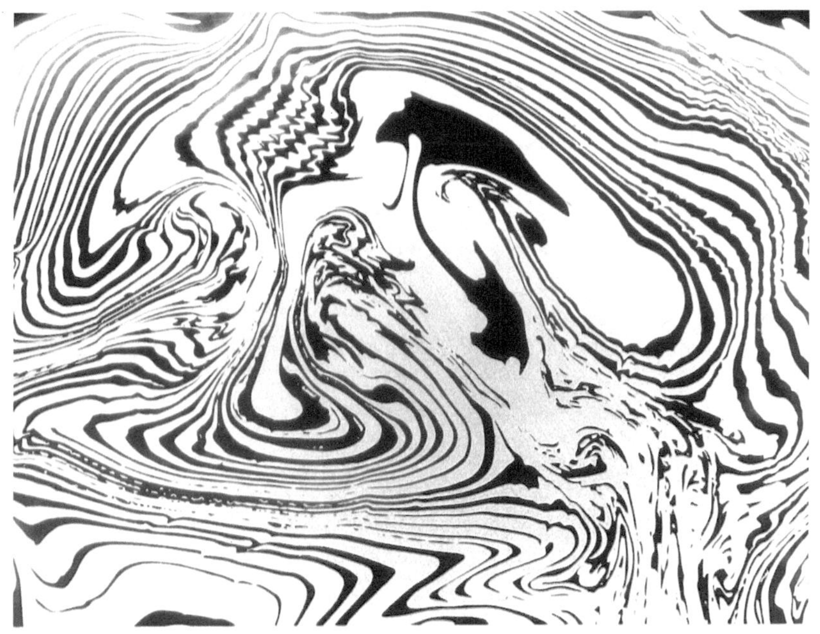

Close-up of the image created by Big Bluestem seeds.

Photo: Courtesy ©Bill Walker

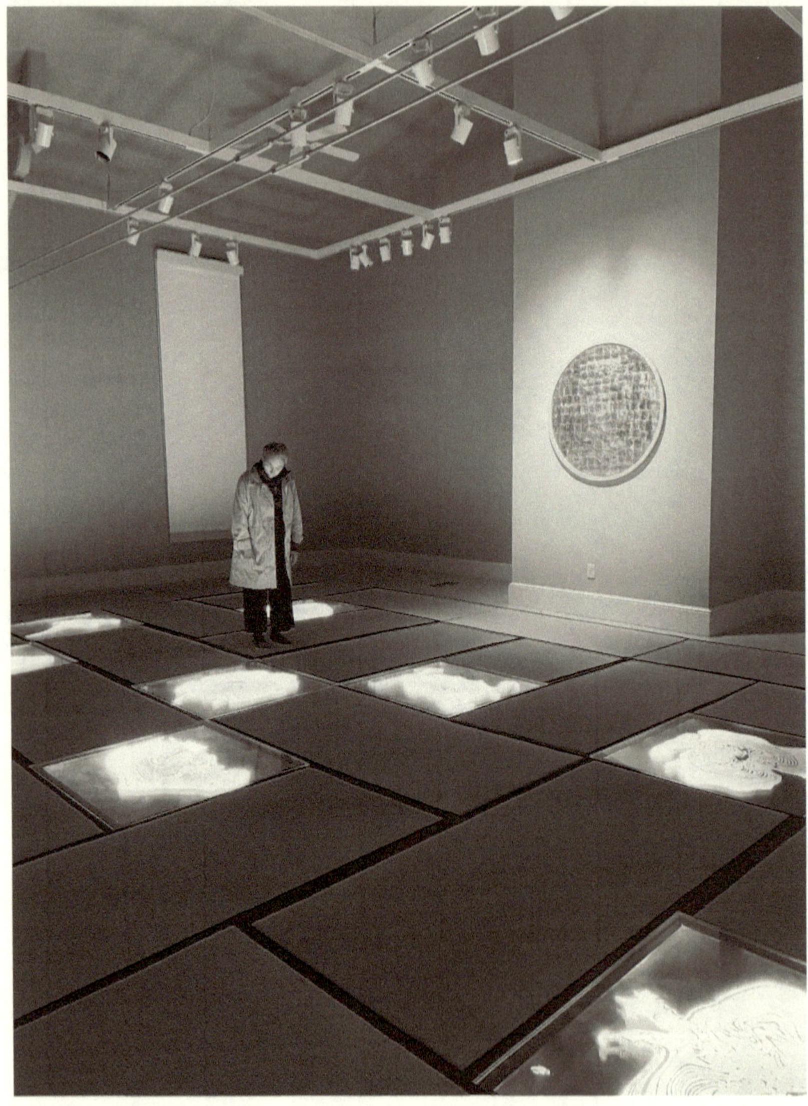

Choreographer and creator of Social Presencing Theater, Arawana Hayashi, takes some time alone with the art.

Photo: Courtesy ©Bill Walker

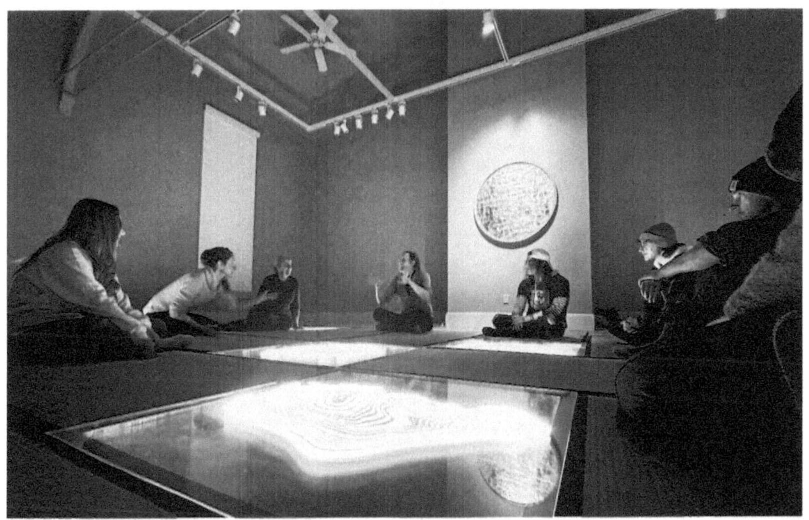

Students from Ohio Wesleyan University engage in conversation with the art.

Photo: Courtesy ©Bill Walker

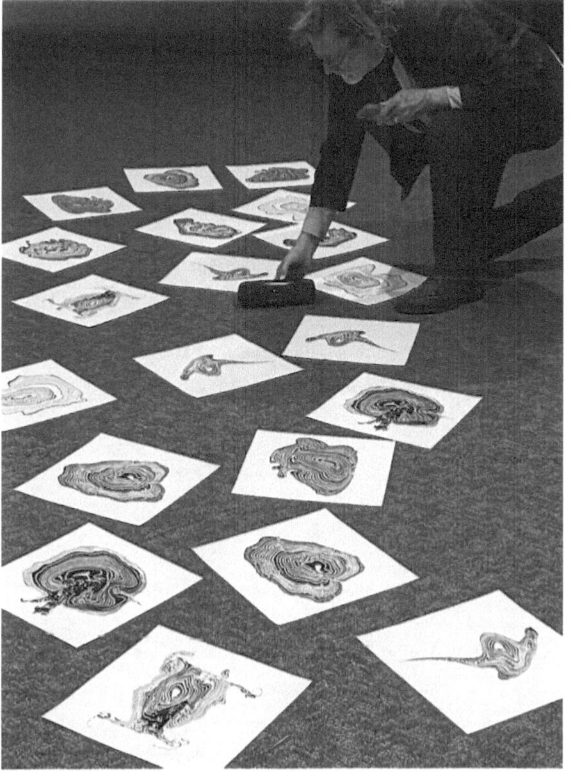

Terry Hermsen arranges prints of the images across a classroom floor.

Photo: Courtesy ©Cadine Navarro

The Nature of Inhabited Space

The real beginning of images...will give concrete evidence of the value of inhabited space, of the non-I that protects the I.

—Gaston Bachelard, *The Poetics of Space*

Walking into *It Sounds Like Love,* one feels welcomed into a kind of *poetics of space.* There's nowhere to turn where one is not *here,* surrounded by the dim light of waking. Or the soothing light of returning to sleep. These glowing panels below us, rising from the floor, pull us like magnets to sit beside them and to listen, touch, extend ourselves—legs, arms, head and torso—till we too are part of the art. From the start, a sequence of waves moves across them, each with its own distinctive explosion of light mixed with sound, image, invention, reflection. In the images produced by the sounds of seeds, fed through the medium of the floating ink, we can often find ourselves taken back to childhood. To the play of light across a wall in an early bedroom, to our eyes blinking as winter dusk settles in, to currents approaching and withdrawing from a beach, to the sounds of the undertow, pulling away.

We are brought back into the nature of inhabiting space. Of roots, memory, homes we once knew, places and crevices where earth-light crept through. Here amidst the seed images, there seem to be endings that never had beginnings. Beginnings that open up trails of long unspoken names and loves.

I'm reminded of the globe game we played as children. Place your finger anywhere. Turn the globe and spin. Repeat. Where will it take you? I've felt the same here, as the lines of the seed patterns fill memory with impossibility. The whole earth behind the walls. Here is my grandmother's cellar. Here her attic door. Here the story of castles and moats and her voice which pulled me and my sisters toward sleep. Maybe the rain is falling again. Or a snowstorm down which we'll slide toward a traffic-less street. I breathe in and out of dream. I follow a wall with my hand extended in darkness, unwilling to find the light switch. Where are the books that will show me the tree-shadows in the backyard? When do I learn to hold them for a full afternoon?

Which is to say: this space of the seeds opens up all spaces. What road we have ever traveled down does not somehow bring us here, even if this *here* does not so much sprout from human stories but rather stories entering earth before humans? Or maybe better yet: the two merging, within our consciousness and beyond our knowing.

A Million-Year Explosion

Somewhere, just a short time before the close of the Age of Reptiles, there occurred a soundless, violent explosion. It lasted millions of years, but it was an explosion, nevertheless. It marked the emergence of the angiosperms—the flowering plants....Neither the birds nor the mammals, however, were quite what they seemed. They were waiting for the Age of Flowers. They were waiting for what flowers, and with them the true encased seed, would bring.

—Loren Eiseley,
"How Flowers Changed the World"

Here we speak that language. The language of seeds, the language of us. The roots of what came before. And as Eiseley puts it, the flowers that through their encased and portable seeds, carried by beak and paw, wind and fur and digestion, spread expansive life across this planet, reaching back something like 140 million years. And stretching to now.

The sweet solitude of this place can hardly be imagined without being here. Pages in a book or a few photographs can hardly convey such peace. It is a place where images allow a dear space to dwell in, to invent, to rearrange our lives.

Do you recall the taste of cherries? Bins of apples that gather in the cellar, wrapped in newsprint, wintering amidst nests of mice? Did you carry nests back to your mother, garnered carefully from pine branches, or the nook of a bent tree? Were there Rose-of-Sharon bushes that still remain in the niches of that yard? Raspberries you harvested but had never planted? In your bedroom of youth, did a fire crackle in a black woodstove just beyond the wall? Was it winter, in the deepest of snows? Is there a nap waiting there now, the walls pressed against the winds? When you touch these channels of ink, which home pulls you in?

Our roots here…sound like love…in time that doesn't constrict…that crosses continents…and many, many homes. Some of them nests…or burrows…swaying high in a tree…tucked under a gutter…drilled into bark… hunkered under ice. Homes that reside beside us…often unseen…that remember routes underground where roots connect…held before us…without absolute differentiation.

At this moment in time, fields and forests all over the earth are burning. In western Europe. Along the richly forested realms of the western U.S. and the southwestern slopes of Canada. Even in the Arctic. And deep in Brazil—to make room for more roads, mining and rootless cattle ranches. Within that knowledge, bring your own roots here. Settle in. The floor invites us to the deepest of stories. Re-beginnings.

From such beginnings, may new prairies grow.

Jester's Journeys

I thought the earth
remembered me, she
took me back so tenderly, arranging
her dark skirts, her pockets
full of lichens and seeds.

—Mary Oliver,
from "Sleeping in the Forest"

With their nearly invisible, elusive presence, so rich but so completely beyond our sense of time and perception, these seeds appear to welcome the voice of the Trickster... or the Jester. How else can we imagine the existential *fact* of them? Illusive as the earth itself, nearly timeless, ubiquitous as stones, these seeds only reveal their sounds when addressed, when invited. As Navarro and Glowski have admitted, at first *no* sound arose, placing the microphone on the seeds. But then they began to speak with them, making heartfelt requests for communication... and the sounds, distinct to each seed type, began, growing steadier and more consistent over time. A magical discovery, woven from playful engagement. A dance, a courtship, an extended hand from a world that at times pulls us in, at times withdraws.

Sometimes, hunkered in here, I hear the Trickster voice sneak around corners, creating lights across a floor that rides like water, conjuring history in a single phrase. If it's *play,* if it's teasing, it's tickling our ears, the trickster's voice of Mary Oliver's night music whispering from within.

Is there such an earth still, to be gained through wandering, through lying down? We long to know, within this space, within ourselves, at whatever age, waiting before the curtain as it's ready to rise, ready to speak. Here I want to find ways to lean closer, to the ripples of roads, paths, branches, patterns in sand. Is there *time* in such a world? In this space where the seeds speak? Where Jester lives?

* * *

Perhaps Jester dwells at the edge of the city. Gardening in caked and stony dirt, up comes a small remnant of a once-flying life, more vibrant than any of *us*, and with it a poem that seems to appear from the ground itself, perhaps to be called, "'How Graceful the Small Before Danger.'"

In overturned dirt by the garden, a bird's skull
Its gaunt lightness
follows me
within my hand.

And if again I wonder can a blackbird
balance on a reed
the answer is within my bones.

There is wind
and there is stone
and in-between
there are the fragile blossomings of life
with fragileness our strength.

At the edge of the seeds, at the edge of a decaying city, Jester walks off into a world we might still imagine.

HOPSCOTCH LECTURE

Carbon dioxide emissions will not change unless everything else that encourages them changes as well.
—Charles Eisenstein, *The More Beautiful World Our Hearts Know Is Possible*

How can art serve earthly renewal? Can it find ways to change our paradigms, bring us to the floor, the land around us, all we have not heard? We'll need our minds and ears, our hands and our wonder, our facts and our dreams, to bring wholeness around. To invite real change.

"Art parallels life," John Dewey said. Through it we get to "experience our experience," as it keeps open in us the ability to take in the world, numb as we can become to the incredible majesty of just being alive on a planet so precious and spilling over with teaming life. Art for him is one of our major ways, if not our primary one, of redirecting ourselves toward engagement, and here he reaches out to all creatures—including the more-than-human. As he writes, "Every living experience owes its richness to what Santayana well calls 'hushed reverberations.'"

Entering *It Sounds Like Love,* as a living art form, I often feel that upwelling of "hushed reverberations" with peripheral ears. From that realm, over and over in people's response to the show, we learn how to reengage the earth again, as we join our own creatureliness with the that of our seed companions.

Jeanette Winterson claims:

> Every day, in countless ways, you and I convince ourselves about ourselves. True art, when it happens to us, challenges the "I" that we are.

She continues:

> A love-parallel would be just: falling in love challenges the reality to which we lay claim, part of the pleasure of love and part of its terror, is the world turned upside down. We want and we don't want, the cutting edge, the upset, the new views. Mostly we work hard at taming our emotional environment just as we work hard at taming our aesthetic environment. We already have tamed our physical environment. And are we happy with all this tameness? Are you?

Winterson says *art objects* to all this tameness. And in an era where we need to open back up to the earth, to re-wild it, as many have claimed, her call to us as artists is all the more intense.

Thoreau writes, "Hope and the future for me are not in lawns and cultivated fields but in the impervious and quaking swamps. I enter a swamp as a sacred space... There is the strength, the marrow of nature."

He speaks of a "tawny grammar," by which he means a kind of "wild and dusky knowledge" that can be found in poetry, or in children's early speech, in reaching beyond the bounds of language. Listen to a one or two-year-old child learning to shape words and sentences, or putting a finger up to dots on old wallpaper and saying, "rain," or riding a tricycle down the street and explaining "I'm pushing in summer." A four-year-old looks up at the sunset and asks, "Where does the dark go when the dark goes down?" That's what I think Thoreau means by "tawny grammar."

He could be talking about the sounds of these seeds.

The Seeds of Poetry

I lean on a song.
I follow a story.
I keep my mother waiting
when she asks, *How long*
before the wren finishes the grain?
How soon until we see
what a house the birds
build by flying? In the dream
in which I stopped with her
under branches, on the long way to school,
one of us, curious
about the fruit overhead, asked:
To what port has the fragrance so lately
embarked, for whose tables?
One of us waited for the answer.
And one went on alone,
singing. And all the place
there was grew out of listening.
—Li-Young Lee, "Build by Flying"

At Heritage Middle School, we read this poem in the inventive, welcoming room-of-inquiry that is the classroom of Mindy Holmes. Among her students are many whose families come from countries all over the world (Somalia, Mexico, India, Sri Lanka, Egypt). It is a joy to bring this poem into their midst. Born in Indonesia, where his Chinese father had been exiled after a run-in with Mao Tse Tung, Li-Young Lee was eventually raised in western Pennsylvania, where his father (after another expulsion for his political beliefs) became a Presbyterian minister. In the presence of this marvelous array of international, multilingual students, telling that story takes on even more relevance. Where do we *all* come from? What are our true "home languages"?

How will we find a place of belonging amongst all our wanderings, in a place that might eventually grow "out of listening"?

So many unknowns, so many unheard worlds surround us. For one, the complex yet simple layers of the Earth, growing ever more intricate the more we observe, listen to, take in, explore the sounds of seeds, the textures of winds, the interchange within roots of trees that in this late time we are just becoming aware of. Add to all that the array of tones, the "twhips and cluspings" that shape our tongues—in so many diverse languages—and we walk without hardly being aware, amidst languages we've never heard, that are quickly disappearing all around the earth.

I ask the class to imagine writing words on slips of colored paper...then heading to the balcony at the school entrance and throwing them over the railing, watching them rain down.

That's how we begin our class on a Monday morning. Later this week these wonderful students will write about Cadine's seed images, but for now we are planting our own language seeds. We fill the slips of multi-colored construction paper with physical nouns and active verbs starting as often as possible with the letters B, D, G, K, P, Q, T and hard C...dove, dive, blanket, globe, pillow, tongue... and forming what we called "creative opposites" on the other side of each word. What's the opposite of pillow? We toss out many options. Feather? Brick? Stream? Each tiny picture built from those various choices opens up the kind of fluid tension that poetry relies on. Thoreau's "tawny language", that will ride on its metaphors and prepositions, as Robert Frost claimed long ago.

Over the balcony of this tiny village of a school, we watch the colors of our words flutter down, recreating a floating dictionary in the air. We write standing up, or lying down between the spaces formed by wherever those slips of paper land—each one in random relation to the others, pressed up next to each other like newly discovered neighbors. Pens in hand, we conjure metaphors for "what our minds are like" (those *other* unknowns whose wonders we barely tap into in our daily lives):

> My mind is like a clock filled with roses
>
> My mind is like kings in the dark.
>
> A universe of coral in traffic
>
> My mind is like a glass
> full of candle wax topped
> off with a blaze of hours
>
> My mind is like a cloud toupee
>
> My mind is like yarn
> Tangled, tortured, terrible
> Terrible, but warm
>
> My mind is like the shadows
> under our shoes

A grand morning. Dancing our minds awake, in preparation for living the mysteries all over again.

Symbol, Play and Festival

> *Play is less the opposite of seriousness than the vital ground of spirit as nature, a form of restraint and freedom at the same time...For these our forms of play are forms of our freedom. Human production encounters an enormous variety of ways of trying things out, rejecting them, succeeding or failing. 'Art' begins precisely there, where we are able to do otherwise.*
>
> —Hans-George Gadamer,
> *The Relevance of the Beautiful*

Experiencing *It Sounds Like Love* is nothing if not an invitation to *play*. And not just in being silly, though many children—and even a number of college students—can't resist rolling around on the seed images, or dancing upon them, moving from one to the other, as if they were a spontaneous game-board. One five-year-old girl, on hearing from her mother what made these images, immediately curled up on top of switchgrass, pretending to be reborn as a seed!

But take it further, as Gadamer suggests. Play is an essential part of all human endeavors, from the way lawyers tweak a statute to open up a fresh interpretation of the law, to the way an actor might play with a typical James Dean or Marilyn Monroe image, making it their own, "tipping our heads" to see what those iconic figures were about. In fact, Gadamer suggests that art gives us three essential features of civilization: symbol, play and festival. Symbols arise as cultural metaphors, the roots of which run so deep into language, from Japanese or Chinese pictograms to the way words like "meander" come from the river Maeander or Meandros in Asia Minor, the way "astronaut" combines "astro" and "nautical" to produce "star-sailor." And then, from such beginnings of creative imagery, he suggests that art *plays* with those images, the way the Eiffel Tower might be said to play with a church steeple, adapting it into the Age of Iron. We are not stuck, in other words, with all the imagery which came before; rather, art offers us the ability to revise how we live.

You could feel it in the atmosphere of our gatherings at the Frank. We couldn't resist. Metaphors for what a particular seed image suggested came almost immediately to our minds and conversations. How could we not? Day after day we would pull on that cloak of playfulness and make the voices of the seeds our own.

Three examples:

One African-American college sophomore, reaching his hand out to trace the expanding circles of "Dogbane," compares it to our situation in society. He says: "Think of it as yourself. This part on the outside rim is what you show everybody that you don't know, you show them certain things, give them certain vibes. But closer in, toward the center, it's what you show your close friends or family. It's close-knit. But here at the center is only what you show yourself…things that you tell nobody."

In that same class, a student with bright orange-dyed hair flipped to one side of her head bends down to explore the nonconformist nature of "Wild Bergamot", saying "I was drawn to this one because of its violent antisymmetry. Every other piece that I see has some form of lateral or bilateral symmetry. But this one is like 'no, I refuse'…"

One high school senior, clearly familiar with the counseling world, traces out the lines of "Echinacea", rising and falling like wrinkles on a map or in a pattern of recovery, but is able to connect what she sees to much more as well: "I saw this part here as the eye at the center of the universe, stretching out, just as everyone has certain paths to follow, until they reach the end. Just as in mental health recovery, the passage isn't linear. And you can see how, if you trace out some of the lines, it goes down but always has a tendency to come back up."

Each of these examples (and there are many more) reveal how invested visitors became, hardly able to resist seeing the images as mirrors to their own experience.

From the symbolic and the playful, we were led to the festive and meditative. Sometimes we *began* there, so that even before we spoke about or explained what we were seeing, Cadine or her collaborator Janice Glowski would ask us to lie down beside (or on top of) the seed images, and "enter our breath." Audiences of whatever size, whatever our ages, seemed immediately comfortable doing something which would feel so unusual anywhere else. With the seeds speaking, the lights dimmed, slowly led into breathing and exhaling, we were invited to relax into a moment of time where clocks or watches no longer applied. Five or even twenty minutes later, we would raise silently upward, with the twitch of fingers, the curl of a wrist, backs stretching, refreshed, reuniting with the vertical potential of our bodies as if we too were growing upward from our seed-status within the ground.

Hunger in Art

It is the business of [art] to embody mystery. And mystery is a great embarrassment to the modern mind. The mystery is the mystery of our position on the earth.

—Flannery O'Connor

Questions glimmer. We arrive in this space, hungry for lives-beyond-our-own. But whose?

Are we, as W.S. Merwin once said, like bees with their abdomens removed, so long used to gorging on honey which does not fill us that we do not even remember what true hunger is?

The first sense here is one of not-quite-knowing-where-we-are. We have to adjust our eyes. What have we left behind?

We've lost so much of the sacred. Do we even know how to walk without endless worry? When was my last true breath? We eat. And we talk. We eat while we talk. But have we done either?

There is a different kind of silence here, with such minimal "input." One subtle sun on the wall, containing all these seeds covered over by thin 24-karat gold leaf, in a kind of seed vault. Nine lit panels below. Segmented mats that that frame our walk. What does it feel like, when the room is lit from below?

When these maps are laid out below us, whose journey is this?

So suddenly, there is laughter. What does it feel like, falling into a many-million-year-old explosion?

Walk a little further, stretch out fingers to follow a pattern. Tracing how that pattern disappears.

We eventually arrive at the edges, where we have nowhere to go. And seem to be in no hurry to get there.

In this space, doesn't standing up seem too far removed?

We bend down, fold our bodies closer. Sense some new knowledge we can hardly name that spills out of our arms like leaves we were reaching down to gather.

We too begin as seeds, breaking out of original dark waters.

The ink spills over our eyes, our fingers. If we are lucky.

We enter a language before speech, before syntax, before humans, before intent.

We have consumed so much. Here we can only invite. Here we can only invent.

A new hunger.

To take this work in, with the other creatures. Who seem to be listening around us. Surrounding us.

As if we are mirrors. As if they are hearts.

Tiny Moments of Song

In a hypothetical "trial of humanity" before all the other creatures on this planet, facing the question of whether we have the "right" to continue, the inimitable ecologist David Orr answers in our defense:

> We are learning the arts of designing with natural systems in ways that give back as much as they take. We are beginning the great transformation from coal and oil to efficiency and sunlight. If granted the right to survive, the difficulties and challenges we face in the years ahead will be many, but the turning point in human attitudes and behavior has begun…But science on its own won't save us in the absence of a renewed sense of the sacred sufficiently powerful to overcome our indifference to Earth, which is to say absent a change of heart. [145]
>
> —David Orr, *Down to the Wire: Confronting Climate Collapse*

The intellectual power that has brought humanity this far threatens the viable life on this planet, including our own. How to turn that around? We need all hands on deck now, as the saying goes, with every individual, every classroom and college, every business venture, every aspect of government to seek ways to steer the ship of humanity toward a reconnection with the planet we so deeply love and have so terribly misused. Ideas and concepts will direct us. But such frameworks are only as good as they guide us toward concise, practical solutions that we apply at every level. That's a massive task, one that can give us pause…and stall us just when we need to move forward the most.

How can a song, a poem, a work of art, even an installation as grounded in the earth as *It Sounds Like Love,* make a difference? Might we find here renewed breath, an inner burst of a tiny song hidden in the seeds?

Listen to this classic haiku from Issa, who wrote in the 17th century about this "tiny moment":

> The man pulling radishes
> pointed my way
> with a radish.

Training the mind to listen to earth may involve many such barely realized moments of sound, song, memory, attention, peripheral sight, peripheral hearing. Maybe haiku, that blessed Japanese tradition of concise speech, provides a place to start. And one that we can soak in, surrounded by the images of seeds, breathing in the aura of the tatami mats, returning to where we begin.

Along the floor of *It Sounds Like Love,* there are many such moments. Looking for maps, here they are, offering perhaps a quieter path, a touch of inner distance, one body approaching another, veering off, recentering. Ready to dance (and sing) more fully in this world. Pointed forward by the flick of a wrist, a swaying radish.

As some have said, haiku open like miniature movies, where we as listeners supply the rest of the story. And the whole world expands, starting with three lines and a compressed limit of syllables. With haiku, we involve ourselves in a naming of senses and emotions that brave out new ways of being. These gems are invitations to awaken breath-with-longing. The kind of longing for worlds we can live in, where we shake off the burden of heavy responsibility—a kind of societally enforced busyness to be always on the move—and step a little more quietly, lowering the human presence to allow the earth back in.

Haiku are breath-in-the-making. As with Basho:

Even in Kyoto—
hearing the cuckoo's cry—
I long for Kyoto.

So often within these tiny songs there is a "you," as the poem is not to some general public, but provides an intimate invitation, a kind of "answering back." And that ultimate "you" may be the earth itself.

May a small song do its part to guide us.

IN THE CIRCLE OF BEINGS

We believe we are at home in the immediate circle of beings. ...But at bottom, the ordinary is not ordinary; it is extra-ordinary, uncanny.

—Martin Heidegger,
"The Origin of the Work of Art"

We might begin to "change everything" by returning to the hardly-realized nature of all that is around us... fetus or clutched hand, an inch of soil, wind in the trees, the touch of a seed or a stone. As Charles Simic did in his poem, "Stone", several decades ago:

Go inside a stone
That would be my way.
Let somebody else become a dove
Or gnash with a tiger's tooth.
I am happy to be a stone.

From the outside the stone is a riddle:
No one knows how to answer it.
Yet within, it must be cool and quiet
Even though a cow steps on it full weight,
Even though a child throws it in a river,
The stone sinks, slow, unperturbed
To the river bottom
Where the fishes come to knock on it
And listen.

I have seen sparks fly out
When two stones are rubbed.
So perhaps it is not dark inside after all;
Perhaps there is a moon shining

From somewhere, as though behind a hill—
Just enough light to make out
The strange writings, the star charts
On the inner walls.

Or maybe look up at the clouds, such as this one above these words right now, its hemispheric turbulence reshaping itself in high and constantly merging patterns? Floating there, seemingly weightless, how could we intuit that its weight would be somewhere near 500 tons?

Jester and Artist drive out to Plum Island Wildlife Refuge, at the edge of the Atlantic. Yael, with her ancient name, a friend of a friend, provides them a three-hour tour, beach to beach, rye grass rotating in all directions along the paths, boardwalks that keep the invading steps of humans away from fragile marshes and dunes. But it's not so much the history that she describes, nor the species she can list, nor the maps she traces out on her hands, showing which designated beach melds into another. Rather it's her love for this expansive world, which her wide arms draw in, the sea breeze that embraces their shoulders on the lookout tower, the coves and inlets, the birch forests, which have just dropped their white-and-red leaves. It's October and the heat of this afternoon will wither soon as the wind picks up.

The friends say goodbye to Yael of the ancient name just at sunset and dart up a last cove. Somehow they know: they've been here before, an hour or a century ago. They're trying to race the sun…and fail. At the top of the last boardwalk, the orange rays have fallen westward, and so they must be content with slip-sliding down the other side, to face the cold and retreating ocean waves. Braced against the wind, tracing the undertow, sharing certain sadnesses, for a long while they hardly look up toward the sky. Then one tips an eye up to notice that the moon has been playing tricks all along, as swaths of clouds slowly drift southwestward, meeting that ancient face and shaping a new optical fantasy each time. The stage of the sky offers scene after temporary scene: a curled sheep, a wilted torch, a miser with his lamp, a coiled hand, two stingrays merging, a shell breaking light out of itself as if it were born there. Each tiny movie lasts a sequence of seconds, before being replaced by the next rush of illusion. Thin, nearly transparent clouds passing slowly across the ivory moon.

As with generations before, they're "watching clouds," but the entertainment is both rapid and stilled, in sudden and frozen flashes of earthly—or heavenly—jubilation, where it's possible to leave the fierce knots of humanness behind, as they stand to face the tides, dance the beach, laughing and circling, grateful for those like Yael who keep guard before the swath of visitors, preserving the hidden names of what glimmers all around.

Heidegger again: "The work of art holds open the Open of the world."

In this time of earthly crisis, how else but in art—and in moments like these—do we face the uncanny and seek ways to "hold open the Open of the world"?

Embodied Metaphor

Once upon a time, words began to vanish from the language of children. They disappeared so quietly that at first almost no one noticed ... acorn, adder, bluebell, bramble, conker–gone! Fern, heather, kingfisher, otter, raven, willow, wren...

—Robert Macfarlane & Jackie Morris, *The Lost Words*

Sometimes it seems to me that with our "normal eyes" we cannot see the river, much less the seeds, the fields, the plants and species we're losing...and that we are so dependent on. I think of a stream which runs through my town but that hardly anyone knows is there. For 700 and more feet, it flows underground through a channel, only becoming visible in spots. On a walk after a meal downtown, we might pause over a small bridge and hear a ripple below, but it's growing late, we rush home, we have things to do.

As with that stream, we wall things off in so many other ways. We talk with a brother we haven't communicated with in years—on any significant level—arguing about a pipeline that threatens the ancient lakes growing native rice, but we do not mention the rice, nor the people who have depended upon that wild expanse for centuries, nor the boreal forests that have been scraped to the ground to squeeze out the sandy oil, an area large enough to set upon the map of England. Our language—our map—cannot hold this to our hearts.

Our "locked-in" eyes dominate us, shaping the range of metaphors we are willing to entertain... and upon which we venture out to face our fears. Will there be a world here, once these years of extraction and seemingly endless war have stripped the earth bare? We can't face that, would rather retreat into convenient games on our little screens.

Maybe it's the Third Eye that will need to do the seeing now. The seed images below our feet, or under the swaying of our hands above them, draw us into an unknown world that seems to have existed years before, the crisp, quiet mutterings of the seeds far in the distance like a memory we never had. Stories, myths that have been waiting in the soil for centuries, stretching back to before we ripped up the prairies and sent the beasts that fed on them into oblivion? Gratefully—if we are ready—we might be brought home.

Sleeping in the Suislaw forest–western Oregon, the conifers rising up a smooth slope, I listen to the wind and read the very poem that I am living in. Surrounded by pines, the darkness settling in like another breath, not fully my own, not fully known, content but not content, unseparated from the long day behind and the quiet night of ease ahead...

Falling asleep the birds are falling
Down through the last light's thatchwork
Farther than rain, their grace notes diminishing
Into that downy pit, where the first bird
Waits to become them
In the midst of the night.

Silent and featherless, now they are
One dark bird in darkness.

Beginning again, the birds are breaking upward
New fledged at daybreak, their clapping wingbeats
Striking the sides of the sun, the spinning brilliant dust
Spun loose on the wind, from the end
To the beginning.

Can I feel David Wagoner's words clicking across the keys? Am I internally aware of what is farther than the rain? I am falling, rising, held within what I am holding, a book, a scattering of words, a resurgence of sounds that know how to be silent at last, knowing they will begin all over, like a breath of time I am beginning to inhale, that inhales and exhales me…"The Death and Resurrection of the Birds."

This is embodied metaphor. Language brought back down to earth. Eyes invested in what my body knows. Or is beginning to know.

Prairie Promise

We work for a future in which humans flourish as members of a thriving ecosphere. Achieving this future requires reconciling the human economy with nature's economy…We consider the distant past and the distant future—tens of thousands of years. We are not daunted by solutions that require decades to realize.

—The Land Institute (Salina, Kansas)

Walk out into a tall grass prairie. Sit inside the we that we are. We who reduced the prairies to one-tenth of one percent of what once covered so much of this continent. Imagine them rising above us now, the bluestem and prairie dock and coneflowers well over our heads. No pronouns here, only sound.

Pick up a brown curled leaf from the base of prairie dock. Scratch its brown surface in your hand, like sandpaper from the ages. In our minds, can we stretch down into a single square foot of bluestem's reaches, which miraculously holds 25 miles of root hairs, rootlets circling to a depth of 7-8 feet? It doesn't take much to dig up this fact, but to plant it in our consciousness requires more than an encyclopedia. We know that entangled, communicative mass fought off the early plows for decades, succumbing at last to double-blade plow and a nation intent on subduing the plains.

Everywhere, the facts are hidden. I've read that certain plants work as "colonizers," spreading toward new territory, adept at adapting to the changing conditions of drought and heat. And that these colonizers make way for "occupiers," which stabilize the prairie over years. We find that prairies sequester carbon more readily than forests, taking only 5-6 years to get reestablished, storing in their soil what would be released when trunks fall and decay. And the ants' work here is invisible too. Some plant species taking advantage of, as one book puts it, "the sweet tooth of ants by providing them with food in return for protection." Sunflowers and partridge peas attract ants by releasing a kind of nectar from their leaves, stems and buds. Then ants feed on the nectar, but also serve to defend the plant from other herbivores. All that creative energy dancing around us too.

Put out your hand. Rub it on the stalk, that somehow doesn't collapse in the first storm of the season. Flex the grit of silicon between your fingers. Or lie down, squeezing yourself between the thick stems. The soil here feels darker than time, seemingly streaked with the weight of meteors. What fed the bison now peaking back up, though their world is mostly gone. Some still dream of its return, of spreading back across renewed prairies the species we have lost, building new soils, recovering plants and systems that might feed us more strongly than our endless application of fertilizers that deplete instead of renew. To feed the table of the future, we might begin with the sounds around us here, the bobolink's chitter, the birds' nests hidden in the expanse, trusting in the luck that being hidden in the mass will be enough protection.

For me, in lying on the floor of *It Sounds Like Love,* all this promise of the prairies lies hidden in the sound of the seeds.

THE LISTEN SEED: INTERNATIONAL STUDENTS MEET *IT SOUNDS LIKE LOVE*

At age 71, near the end of his storied life, winner of the Nobel Prize for Literature, Pablo Neruda began asking questions like a child again:

> Where did the full moon
> leave its sack of flour tonight?
>
> If the color yellow runs out
> with what will we make bread?
>
> How many bees are there in a day?
>
> Who can convince the sea
> to be reasonable?

—Pablo Neruda,
from *The Book of Questions*

On the final day in Mindy Holmes' "international classroom" at Heritage Middle School, we bring Neruda's playful last book into the classroom, reaching back in time and across the hemisphere to discover a new way of experiencing the basic elements of the world. Then we bring out large-size reproductions of Cadine's seed images to fill every desk. Slowly we begin exploring her art and—to the students' surprise—Cadine herself joins us.

As she stands before them, the students get to hear a bit of *her* life story—of having her senior year in high school ended by a massive earthquake that destroyed the town in Japan where she grew up, the sheer shock of the piano in her house being thrown across the room as the walls shook. A sound none of us will ever be likely to witness or convey. And then, in contrast, as she plays the sounds of the seeds, the room becomes stiller than any 8th grade classroom I've ever witnessed. The seeds make sounds? One can absorb the incredulity of these engaged student faces. We all close our eyes to listen more carefully. We lean in. But in some way, it's the sound of ourselves that we are approaching.

Then as they listen to the quiet sounds of the seeds, they hold images from the suminigashi in their hands, turning them all four directions, finding there is no up or down, and move on to the "essential art of questions," as exemplified in Neruda, as he teases us with impossibilities, which may well be the secret doorway to knowing the earth's true wonder.

With these tools of playfulness, of art at its most serious core, the students bring their pens and pencils to paper, entering the seed images as if they were maps to other lives. Deeply taking in Wild Bergamot, Big Bluestem, Milkweed, Little Bluestem, Black-eyed Susan, Butterfly Weed, Echinacea, Dogbane and Switchgrass, they write:

The deeper I look into you
the more vague you become
The edges of your shape stretch
    as if longing for more
yet your abstract center stays put where it
    is, part of it at least
A chunk seems to be melting away
You seem to be screaming
as you lose a part of yourself
It's a liquid-like state that wants
    to be someone else
Or maybe the texture turns into a tree
Wide and short sitting on top of a dream

—Rodav

Sometimes I feel like a pot of water
soon to overflow
feeling tight and enclosed inside my own bubble
faces overwhelm me
Sometimes I feel complicated
on which path I should flee
going every direction trying to find the one
what best suits me
I feel like an unknown seed
What will I become
What will the others in my garden think of me
Sometimes I feel too much,
Sometimes I don't have time to heal

—Nandita

Distorted.
That's what I am?
I think?
I'm something.
An anomaly.
A whisper. A secret.
I have eyes?
Or not.

—Lama

I listen, as the children pass by
I listen as the flower above sways
with the wind
I listen as the couples pass

I listen as all the people continue to leave
Still taking me with them
But I listen
I, the listen seed

— Sydney

Up and out
My nose lifts to scent
Of Earth
Crumbs of dinosaurs and
Dreams
Long forgotten

The spring of my winter
Chatters about what is
Yet to be

Lengthening
Lengthening

My bones stretching
My chest open
My arms wide

I welcome
The guest of my
Future

—Janai

If Gadamer's idea of art as festival can enter a classroom, such were those mere 42 minutes. It felt like going to a movie or a dance, a concert of the seeds blended with a museum come into our midst. The symbols created by the seeds came to life again, as if they'd been set free from their glass and welcomed being held in these young hands. As festival invites us to gather together, we celebrate our connectedness, our joys and sorrows, and the moments of our days enmeshed with time as they evolve and expand. "The guest of *our* future"? They knew it beyond knowing. To my mind, what these students at Heritage Middle School were engaged with, writing their inventive poems about Cadine's seed art, involved a kind of intuitive borrowing from the playfulness of Neruda's questions. But I think their poems also harken back a few days to Li-Young Lee's dream-story with his mother on the way home from school. From those models they found their own way into metaphor-making, as they grappled with what the earth was offering us in these images. It was an immersion for us all—for the students, for Mindy, for me, maybe even for Cadine herself, as we watched their wonder shine.

Spool of Knowing

In 2009 Paolo Lugari, founder of the Columbian sustainable living experiment Las Gaviotas, wrote that "We are not confronting an energy crisis, but one of imagination and enthusiasm."

—Rob Hopkins, *From What Is to What If: Unleashing the Power of the Imagination to Create the Future We Want*

Stretching out, catching breath, the comforting mats, the seeds calling with their unnamed, unexplained voices—what else can we call them but voices—a crackling in the air, the floor becoming a version of earth below us, lifted as we are by a mist of light, where our faces turn toward each other, or our soundless wonderings, wondering what it would be like to lie here the whole night, and what illusions or allusions might appear, tipping in and out of sleep, the Trickster at our side, the words of a poem soothing but turning themselves inside out, in an array of myth-assumption, spirals of plenty, emptiness of want, failures forgotten or embraced, faces we never thought were ours, histories that take on our clothes, creatures below our feet, glimmers peering in and flying off, the worries of a planet stretching out, beyond hopeless, asking us to move, to not rise up again until we *know,* that in this moment which stretches so far beyond us, there's a call forward, a decision to be made, collectively, individually, willingly or reluctant, tumbling down tunnels, facts falling down the sides of wells, water far below, caresses we've given or withheld, candles surrounding us in a circle, as we try on new souls, souls the earth has laid out for us, long before we came here, roots and trunks and boles, solid or swaying, brought here by chance or choice, opportunity or subtle sensing, luck or desire, calling us by name.

Here's a poem I came to love years ago, from Carolyn Forché's first book, appropriately named *Gathering the Tribes*,

"Song Coming Toward Us"

I am spirit entering
the stomach of the stones.

Bowls of clay and water sing,
set on the fires to dry.
The mountain moves
like the spirit of southeast morning.

You walk where drums are buried.
Feel their skins tapping all night.
Snow flutes swell ahead of your life.
Listen to yourself.

I am spirit living
thin wooden years
around the aspen.

You live
like a brief wisp
in a giant place.

Lying here, living this poem again, maybe we can stretch in the bowl of the mountains, the stories of forests, the songs of prairies. Here is the soul of the earth. Of these seeds. Of the beauty we will need, to see ourselves—and all our creaturely kin—through.

A former student, now a friend, Amelia Gramling, writes me a note, after reading *The Hidden Life of Trees* and absorbing all the surprises therein, the way acacia trees pass along messages to each other, as giraffes approach, warning the next trees down the row to send out the old familiar poison which will churn the munching away. The way fungi feed messages underground, linking roots to roots. A vision of connectedness (versus-survival-of-the-fittest) so many of us find inspirational for our times. She writes:

> I've always been invested in structures and scaffolding bigger than me—seeking out ways that planets and planes align. It seemed to me natural that the way to preserve this planet and all its achingly delicate connecting architecture is through a gesture or a poem equally vast and commanding. But now that the world has never felt bigger or more remote, untethered, spooling at all edges, I don't want to make something so wide; I'm not interested in contributing to the collective heaviness. I want to act small and right where I am. I know it can't be one tree or one pipeline at a time, but maybe we each wrap ourselves around one part and pull.
>
> There are 400 trees for every human being. But that ratio narrows every day. Let's start spooling the other way.

Maybe our earthly souls are beginning to learn "spooling". We spool within the seeds, from prairie sounds to living prairies. The leap is not far, but the arc is immense. And maybe Jester leads the way. Walk in, lie down and listen. Step out, plant, build a wood duck box, sit amongst the grasses, track every sound, measure the numbers of species arriving. Sink down to your boots. Trek through the deep rich mud of the renewed wetlands. The calls outward, the calls within.

Seeking the edge of beauty. In all its forms. From that spark, the seeds return. There's a song coming toward us.

THE RELEVANCE OF BEAUTY

The Great Khan said: "It is all useless, if the last landing place can only be the infernal city, and it is there that, in ever-narrowing circles, the current is drawing us." And Polo said: "The inferno of the living is not something that will be; if there is one, it is what is already here, the inferno where we live every day, that we form by being together. There are two ways to escape suffering it. The first is easy for many: accept the inferno and become such a part of it that you can no longer see it. The second is risky and demands constant vigilance and apprehension: seek and learn who and what, in the midst of inferno, are not inferno, then make them endure, give them space."

—Italo Calvino, *Invisible Cities*

Art, like beauty, has for so long been put on a pedestal, perhaps wandered through in a gallery on a Sunday afternoon, or placed on a wall to make a room more colorful. Rarely seen. Or known. Go to an art opening in any local gallery and watch how many people are paying more attention to the free wine than to what is on the walls or before their eyes. But what if there were something more, a "relevance of the beautiful," an essential significance to our symbol-making, our deep play, our festivals of gathering? Can we learn from art what we cannot find elsewhere? Can it, with renewed, spun wonder, offer a public space where we come together for engagement, a kind of transformative hoop we need to pass through—toward what is not inferno? We need all the committed engineers, planners, theorists, teachers, farmers and urban designers we can find, to truly face what is before us. But somewhere around the edges, or at the center, we might need art, or whatever tries on its clothes.

What if such art brought us to the brink of change? What if it gave us new myths and stories to live through, embracing the earth with a fierce but buoyant intent? As here, in Susan Mitchell's poem called "Blackbirds":

> Because it is windy, a woman
> finds her clothesline bare, and without rancor
> unpins the light, folding it into her basket.
> The light is still wet. So she irons it.
> The iron hisses and hums. It knows how
>   to make the best of things.
> The woman's hands smell clean. When she
>   shakes them out,
> they are voluminous, white.
>
> All night my hands weep in gratitude
> for little things. That feet are not shoes.
> That blackbirds are eating the raspberries.
> That parsley does not taste like bread.
>
> From now on I want to live
> only by grace. In other words, not to deserve things.
> Without rancor, the light dives down
> among the turnips. I eat it with my stew.
>
> Today the woman's hands smell like roots. When she
> shakes them out, they are voluminous, green.
> All day they shade me from the sun.
> The blackbirds have come to sit in them.
> Since this morning, the wind has been enough.

In some way I can't quite explain, I am transformed by this poem. Playful as it is—or maybe because of its playfulness—we get to feel the wind again, the joy of light "diving down amongst the turnips," the sense that we don't have to (and truly can't) *control* everything. And along with Rob Hopkins I start to wonder: *what if*...what if we could change how we see and shape our relationship with all that we share this planet with—even the land, maybe especially with land? Can we shake up what we experience "in common," and all the boundaries we place around our daily lives? The expectations that have led us to such destructive practices, as we back ourselves into a corner of demise?

One local example of "what if?" can be found in the story of Jim Reding's environmental studies classes in Granville, Ohio. Making use of his major assignment for the year, which he calls a "Take Action" project, his students are finding means of answering the climate crisis back. One fall it came to their attention that the farm beside the nearby intermediate school was for sale. They began wondering what would happen if that land was bought up for development, resulting in yet another random subdivision…and they created a plan to seek funding to save at least part of that acreage.

Jim Reding reflects: "Seven years ago, there were 43 acres of corn and bean fields next to Granville Intermediate School. That's where the students decided to do their work. As part of these projects, they typically have to come up with funding. They enlisted the help of several people, including Brent Sodergren from the US Fish and Wildlife Service, to come out and go over their plan. Based on their conversation with Brent, they ended up taking on a much grander challenge. From an original plan to work with four or five acres, we ultimately ended up with a Land Lab covering over 40 acres. What was once corn and bean fields is now prairies, forest complexes, wetlands, and vernal pools. It's a thriving ecosystem. In a matter of two years, we were seeing diversity there that we didn't even expect to see. Today, we have around 100 acres of Land Lab with nine different habitats. We've planted well over 2,000 trees. We have 30-some flowering plants in our prairies."

Such exciting transformations don't happen without asking "What if?" What if they tried to get 4-5 acres of that land...and pursued it? What if the students went to the School Board to ask for a commitment... and spent six months going back, arguing for this "added value" to their education? The story goes that it came down one May to a final vote. One student got up—Dustin Braden, a fine observer of wildlife, a superb photographer and future environmentalist—and asked, "Well, are we going to do this or not?" The rows of young faces around the room supplied the answer. But it didn't come without dreaming, without wondering, without persistence. Because of that beautiful persistence, the students—and parents, teachers, school board members, administration and indeed the whole community of Granville—will have this learning-space for years to come.

Starting where we are. In mid-Ohio. In the erased prairies of Kansas. Along the edge of our midwestern great lakes...among the largest in the world but hardly known as anything more than places to launch barges or retreat for a brief holiday. Can we come to know the seeds of change? What will it take to listen? Activist Joe Brewer says, "Our globalized economy is built on the commodification of nature. It treats places as sources of extraction that feed globalized supply chains. A key learning process is the rediscovery of ways to live in local places that cultivate deep personal identification with specific landscapes ...weaving into a tapestry of diverse projects. Every region of the earth is filled with seed kernels of possibility."

The seed kernels of possibility. I believe we hold them in our hands.

Part Three: Songs for the Seeds

From Cadine Navarro's Public Artwork, *It Sounds Like Love*

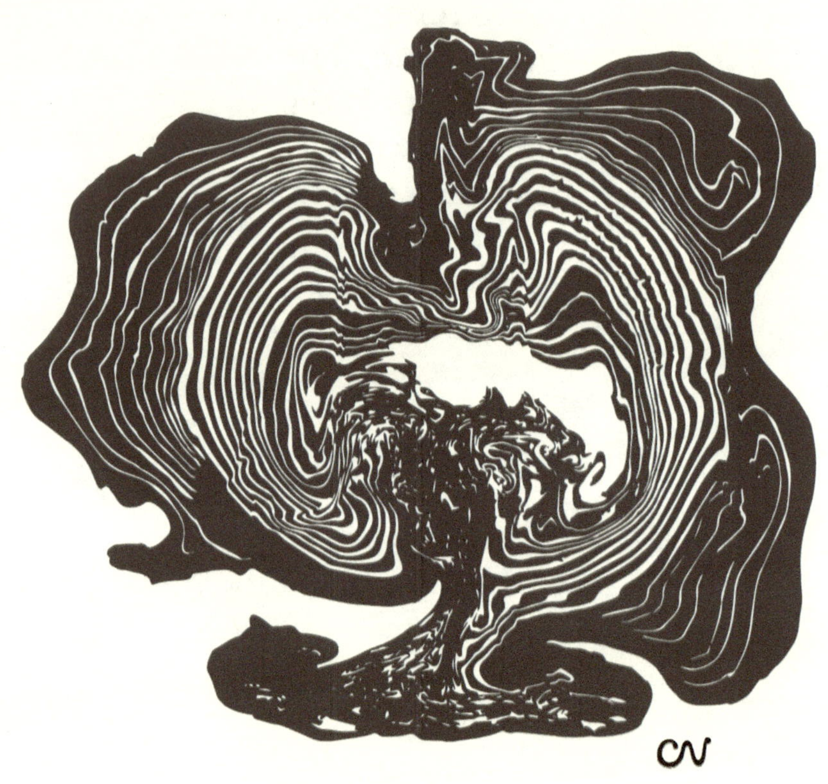

Milkweed

I do not know
what explosion
spun you awake

or what dark boat
began your first sail

Were there tears
that formed inside of—and which—
caves—

and did you hear
the earth turn
toward a shepherd's moon?

I don't know the moment
when all your faces
echoed through each other

into breath

like a beak cracking open
the whiteness
of clutched shell

swimmer within
earth pressure wound
your neck still curled, cooling

in your eyes pulled toward
sleep again

Skin of mother—
child dispersed

Arise, seed

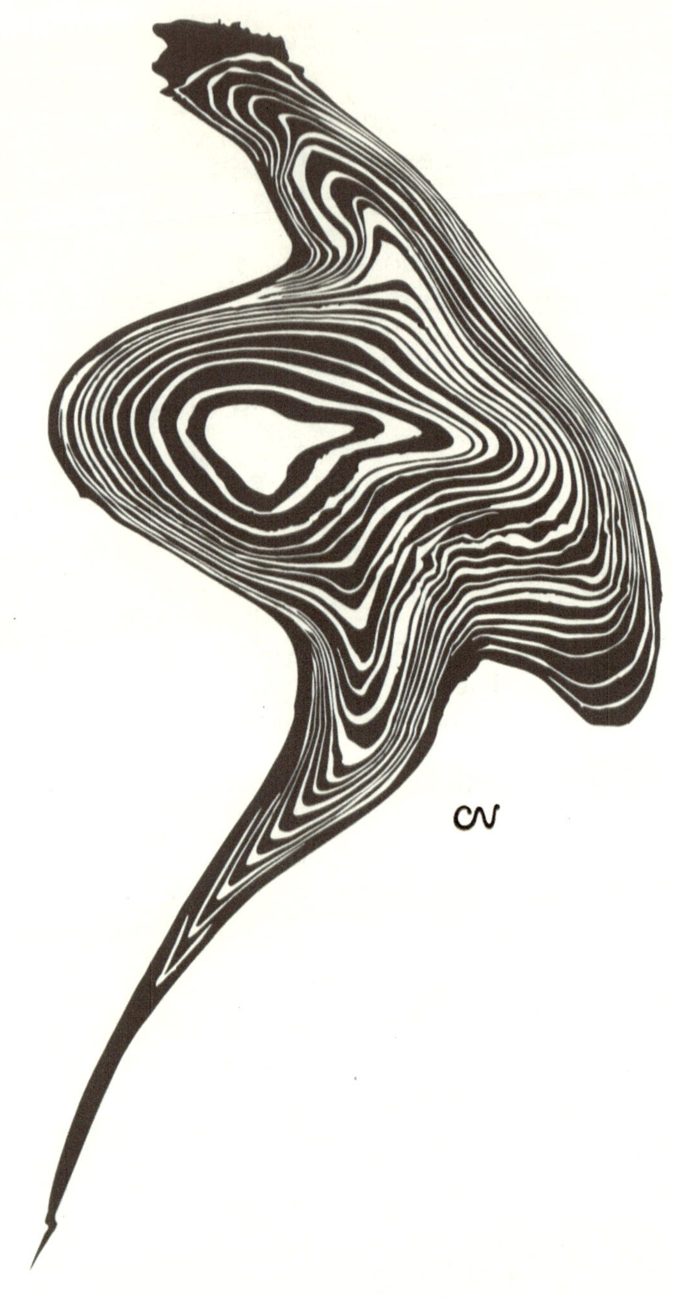

Switchgrass

Seeking soil do you lie down
where wind has sculpted
a bed

—

and must the arch of the mountain
offer you its first born
mooring?

—

I think you drink
from a well and then
fold yourself to fit

—

some elegant scroll

—

Already your numeral
predicates ripple
in me

—

as I lay you around
my shoulders
and wear the day

—

you have named

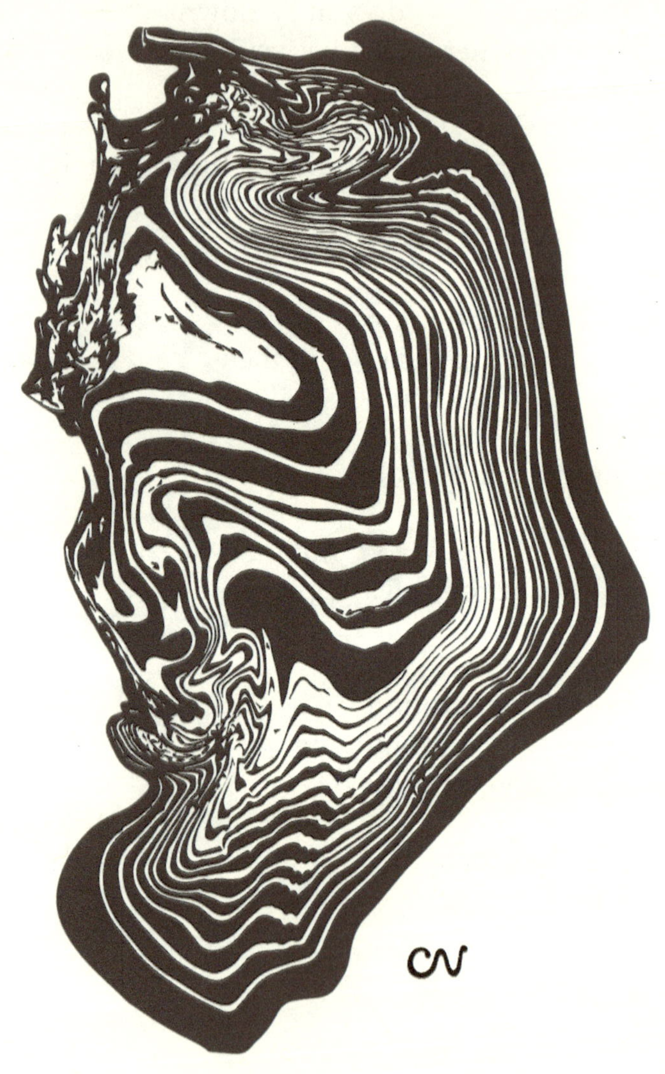

Wild Bergamot

If you speak   four winds
  will you lend me one

 for a pillow

cavern sealed over
        by skin

       now that you are shedding both
        name and story?

You who hold portent

 who have fed me
         beak by beak

       I lay my head down as close
to the angle
         of your ridge   as you will allow

empty harbor, ship with its own
            waves   bend me,
         dear spine

till one day my roots too
         are ready   for burning

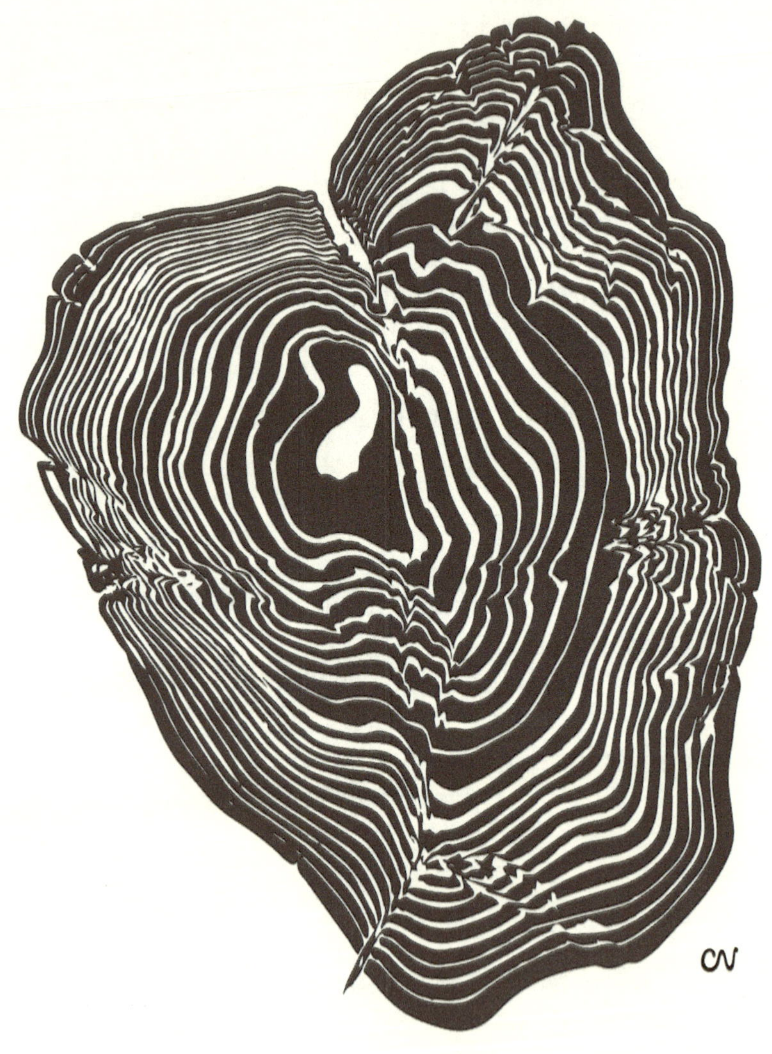

Butterfly Weed

Bird—are you practicing this day again?
—
Pattern—do you reach in?
—
Crater—does rain elude you?
—
Tongue—do you taste turn?
—
Breathing bond—do you speak open?
—
Bordered story—did song collapse?
—
Ridges ridden
—
Pyramid piety
—
break
break
break
break
break
—
the whole of me
—
here is need

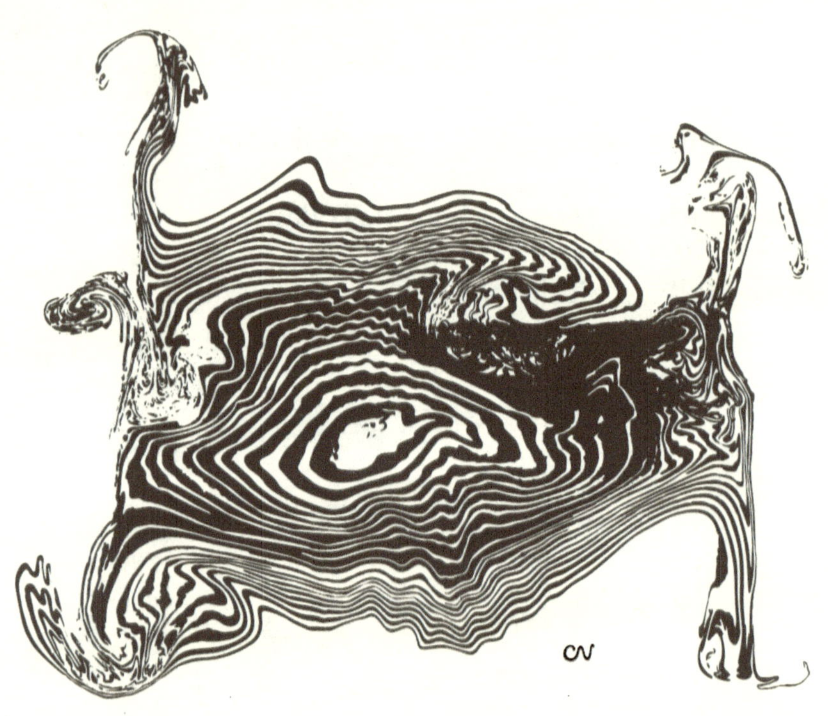

ECHINACEA

Goat mind   tasseled jester
  sleep beside me   would you
    for a year

—

Do you love the waves
  of your body as much
as I do?

—

When you sing do you
reach out   and loop the sound
back   before

—

it latches flame?

—

Here a whirlpool
  for a foot

—

Here a belly
  to tickle the brine

—

Before you were seed
  you curled millennium
    around   fetus pinkie shrine

—

did you

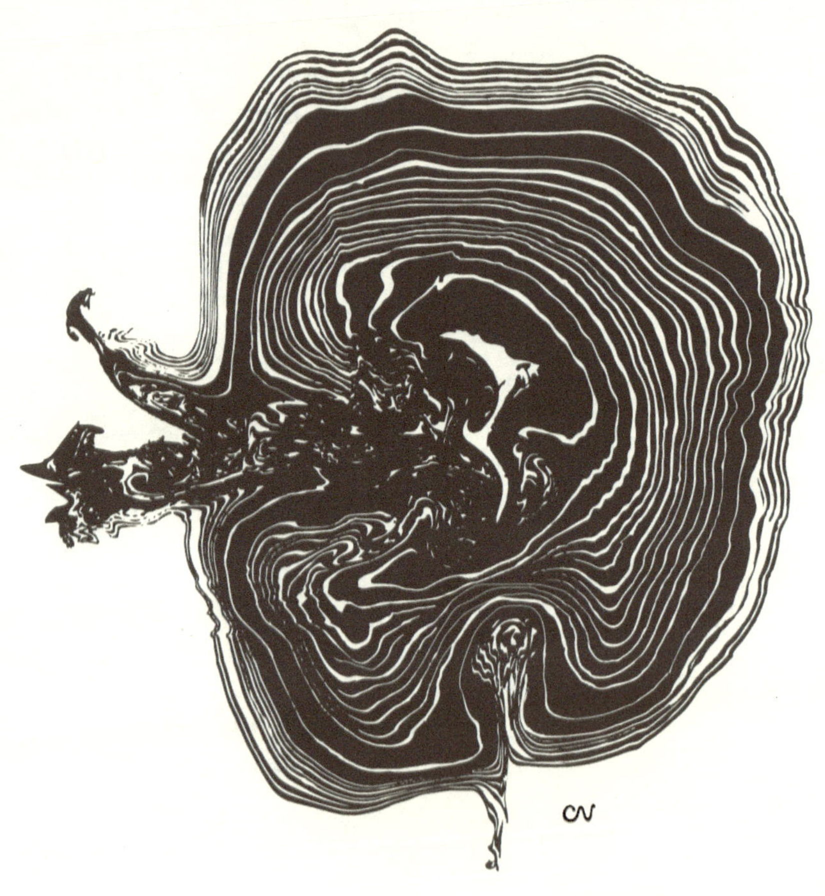

Black—eyed Susan

If you called me again
after chaos   after the street
full of sultry voices
—
has sunk
—
and you fold into my hand
would there be some laughter
of swirled momentary
—
return
—
each one of your
ripples—breath torn token—
another century scraped
—
into sand?
—
I'm learning to walk   again
over chasm
but each day I cradle
—
a glowing face swirl
spree
ready to sign its name
—
genie grant me
your wish

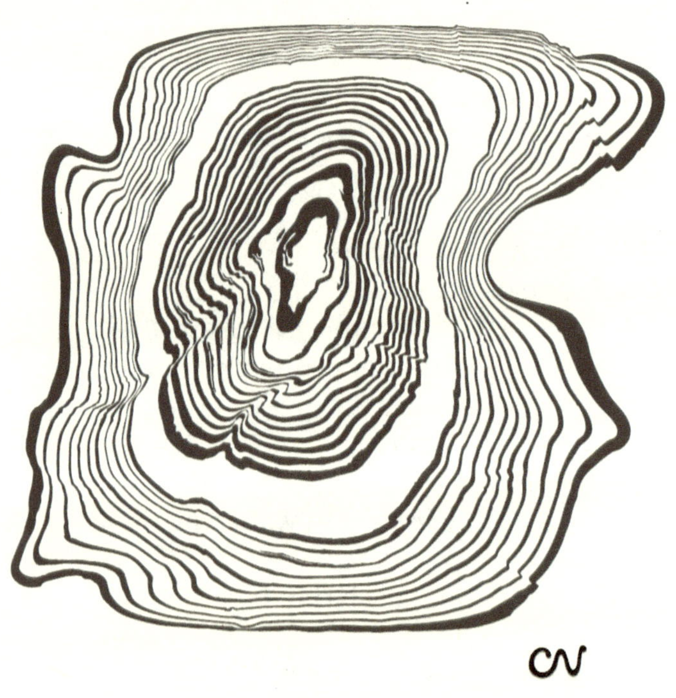

Dogbane

Yes, I will turn away now
friendship is moaning

—

Given an hour I will take ten

—

Bend to the valley
    of enter

—

Here is a spine—fold it
    under me

—

It's taken me years
to be whole as a hive

—

Each one of my wrinkles
    another passage

—

rock hum seek gift
    pulling back

—

grieving lion will you
    cram for a home

—

will you pull me round
    for a face?

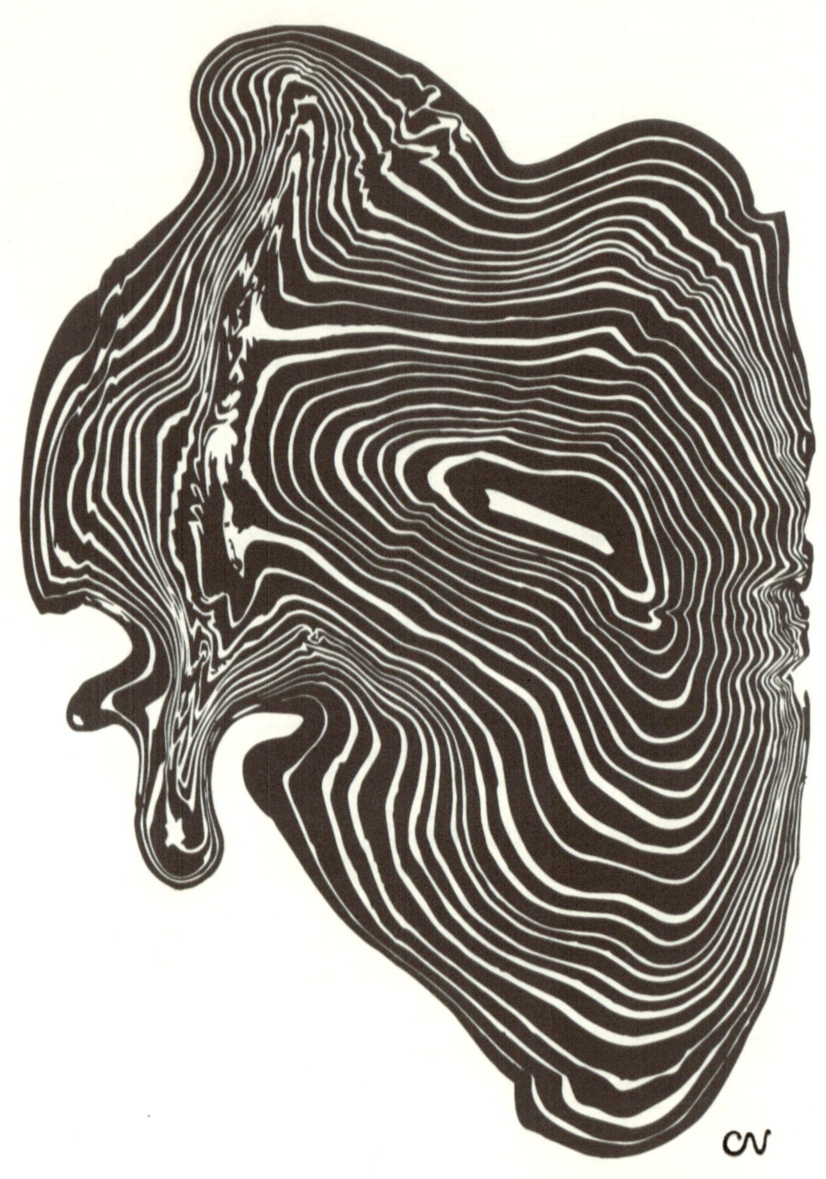

Little Bluestem

When you tell me there's time
I pause a moment
before I lick your eyelid

—

your lashes tickle
your duck blind mind
winks back

—

Hermancita   I will wait
you hold so many
wishes and wills

—

My prairie is lush
with how you bend

—

Most days I rise to your
tunnel wonder   and pretend

—

I can burrow through
the trails
you leave

—

but no   they are
too close to the ground
and I fall back

—

to first memory   of dark

—

please   wriggle   your fingers

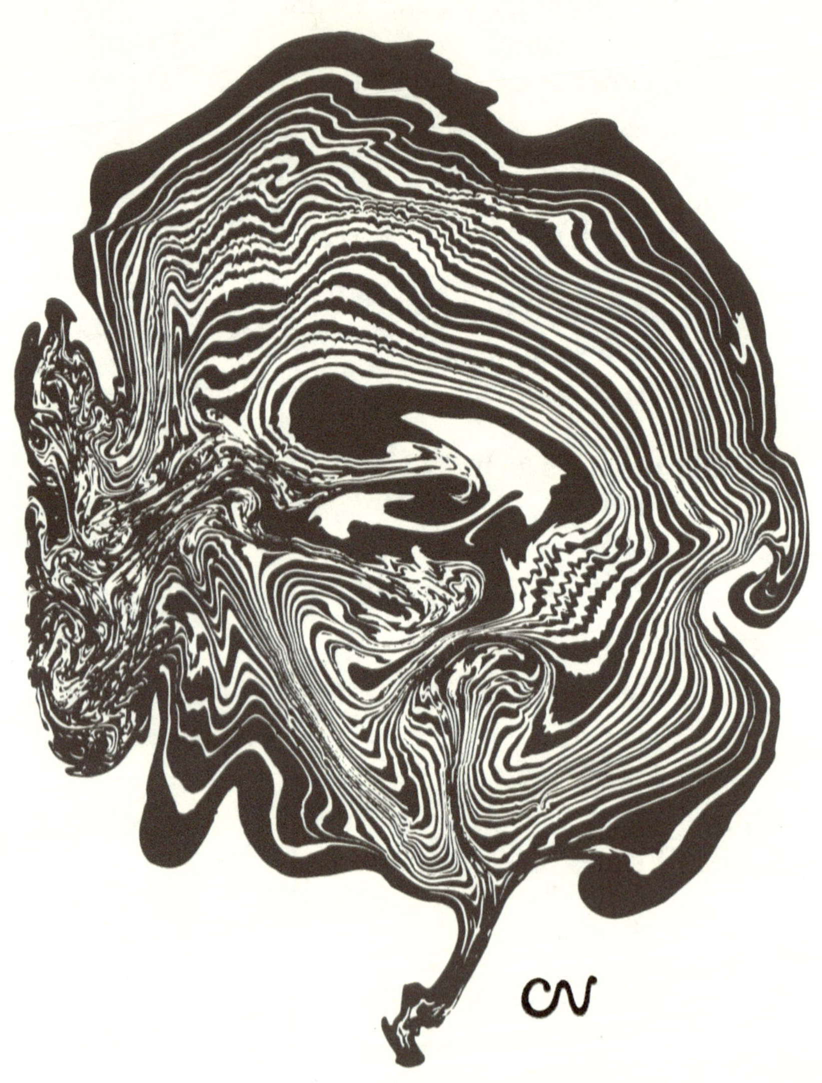

Big Bluestem

I wonder if you will sing with me now
no matter where my eyes are

—

I have tried on so many
mirrors of you I have forgotten
where you last lay down

—

Riven heart
Sea hammer
Strands of your jagged hair

—

I am learning to sit
and not wonder why

—

Nothing begins without
your forest spilling on

—

Nothing ends if I don't bend
and ask you in

—

Dear sage was right I will float
on now and never

—

know where I am
where I am not

Acknowledgements

First of all, my humble thanks to these three dear friends who lent their artistry, thoughtfulness and support in bringing Cadine Navarro's public artwork *It Sounds Like Lovė* to life in all that happened there:

Cadine Navarro, whose beautiful artwork this is... and within whose vision our gatherings at ISLL grew. The many conversations we had, both in and out of the gallery, led in so many direct and indirect ways to my reflections in this book. My heart-felt thanks!

Janice Glowski, curator for *It Sounds Like Love* and Director of the Frank Museum of Art at Otterbein University, who worked tirelessly to create and promote ISLL... and lent our time in that space its special quality of attention and care. This wouldn't have happened without you!

Bill Walker, musician, photographer, videographer and lifelong friend, who spent many hours playing flute and drums for our gatherings, photographing and videoing those events, and lending his vision as well into what ISLL meant for us all. With you, we created such a dynamic quartet!

And so many other people around central Ohio played crucial roles, including but not limited to:

- Michelle Wibblesman and Mark Hoff from Ohio State University's Latin American Studies Department; Jeremy King, Sustainability Director for Denison University; Dave Heithaus, Director of Green Programs at Kenyon College; and Dionne Custer Edwards, Head of Learning and Public Practice at the Wexner Center for the Arts, all of whom offered financial support for Cadine's Land-Based Artist Residency in central Ohio in the spring semester of 2022, and who brought many of their students to see ISLL.
- Sandy Libertini and Leigh Ann Miller, from the Grange Insurance Audubon Center, who arranged for ISLL to have its second installment there in the spring of 2023.

- Chiquita Mullins from the Ohio Arts Council, who supported our outreach into area schools.
- Amy Shuman, from the Folklore Center at the Ohio State University, who helped us articulate the nature of play as it applied to the exhibition.
- Michael Mercil, artist extraordinaire from the Ohio State University, who showed us the value of ISLL's "radical horizontality" vision.
- Baba Jubal Harris, Ohio-based musician, who filled the Frank Museum with the rhythm of his drums.
- Jon-Paul d'Aversa, energy specialist and owner of Unpredictable City, who told us early on that this art could serve as a *kirtan* for wider ecological knowledge and action.
- Laurie Anderson, Tammy Birk, Bethany Vosberg-Bluem, Nick Kawa, Miceala Vivero and so many other faculty from Ohio Wesleyan, Otterbein, Ohio State and Denison Universities who brought their students to be immersed in the art.
- Jenny Adkins from MAD Scientist Associates, and Rich Bradley from the Ohio State University in Marion, who taught us about prairies and their great diversity.
- Ada and Eliza Adkins, four and six years old, who taught us how to dance with the seeds.
- Joe Campbell and Cecil Okotah from the Environmental Professionals Network, who helped foster a link between this art and the wider environmental community.
- Mindy Holmes from Heritage Middle School, and Leah Rollings from John Glenn High School, who invited us into their schools to teach about the seeds.

Finally, I would like to thank Larry Smith, founder of Bottom Dog Press, for his 40-year support of my work, and the thoughtful way he edited this book, offering meticulous guidance all along the way. And to Susanna Sharp-Schwacke for her design and attention to detail and nuances that brought this book to life.

Works Cited

Bachelard, Gaston. *The Poetics of Space*. Boston: Beacon Press, 1964.

Brewer, Joe. www.slideshare.net/joebrewer31/guiding-the-emergence-of-humanity's future

Calvino, Italo. *Invisible Cities*. New York: Harcourt, 1974. Translated by William Weaver.

Dewey, John. *Art As Experience*. New York: Capricorn Books, 1934.

Forché, Carolyn. *Gathering the Tribes*. New Haven: Yale University Press, 1976.

Eiseley, Loren. *The Immense Journey*. New York: Vintage Books, 1956.

Eisenstein, Charles. *The More Beautiful World Our Hearts Know Is Possible*. Berkely: North Atlantic Books, 2013.

Gadamer, Hans-George, *The Relevance of the Beautiful*, Cambridge: Cambridge University Press, 1985.

Hass, Robert, translator. *The Essential Haiku: Versions of Basho, Buson, & Issa*, Hopewell, NJ: Ecco Press, 1994.

Heidegger, Martin, "The Origin of the Work of Art" in *Poetry, Language, Thought*. New York: Harper & Row, 1971.

Helzer, Charles. *The Ecology and Management of Prairies in the Central United States*. Iowa City: University of Iowa Press, 2010.

Klein, Naomi. *This Changes Everything: Capitalism vs. The Climate*. New York: Simon & Schuster, 2014.

Macfarlane, Robert and Morris, Jackie. *The Lost Words: A Spell Book*. Toronto: Anansi International, 2018.

Manning, Richard. *Grassland: The History, Biology, Politics and Promise of the American Prairie*. New York: Penguin Books, 1995.

Mitchell, Susan. *The Water Inside the Water*. New York: Harper & Row, 1983.

Neruda, Pablo. *The Book of Questions*. Port Townsend, Washington: Copper Canyon Press, 1991. Translated by William O'Day.

Norberg-Hodge, Helena. *Local Is Our Future: Steps to an Economics of Happiness*. Local Futures, 2019.

Oliver, Mary. *Twelve Moons*. New York: Little and Brown, 1979.

Orr, David. *Down to the Wire: Confronting Climate Collapse*. New York: Oxford University Press, 2009.

Thoreau, Henry David. *The Portable Thoreau,* ed. Jeffrey Cramer, 2012.

Wahl, Daniel Christian. *Designing Regenerative Cultures*. Axminster, England: Triarchy Press, 2016.

Wohlleben, Peter. *The Hidden Lives of Trees*. Vancouver: Greystone Books, 2015.

About the Author

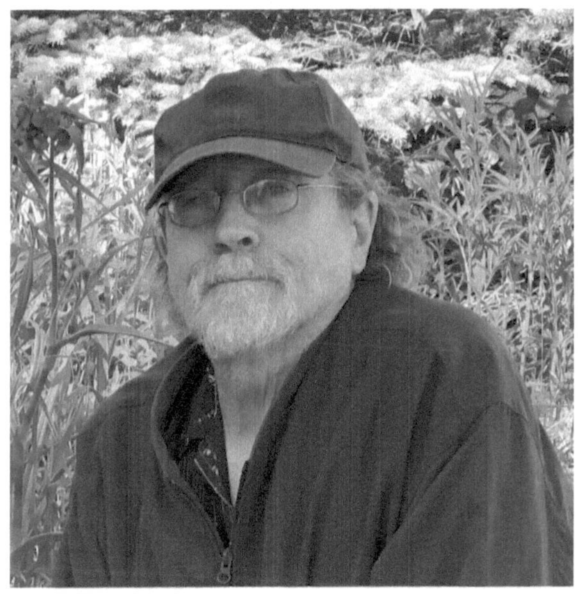

Terry Hermsen grew up in Illinois and Michigan. His poetry has always been tied to his life experiences. In 1976, at the age of 26, he and his first wife Carla rode their bicycles across the country—an experience which led to his first book, *36 Spokes: The Bicycle Poems* (Bottom Dog Press's second volume in 1985). After that, he and his wife moved to Plymouth, Ohio, where they homesteaded for five years—and had a daughter named Isa. This experience led to his second book, *Child Aloft in Ohio Theatre,* ten years later in 1995. A move to Westerville, where they lived on the banks of Alum Creek, evolved into his third book, *The River's Daughter,* which was co-recipient of the Ohio Poet of the Year Award in 2009. His fourth book was *A House for Last Year's Summer* in 2017, greatly influenced by his time teaching in museums and his study of art education in his PhD work at Ohio State University.

He taught for the Ohio Arts Council for over 20 years, visiting schools across the state and conducted poetry night-hikes in over a dozen state parks. He taught literature and writing at Otterbein University from 2003 to 2017. Over the past six years, Terry has helped to found a group called ROAR: Regional Ohio Action for Resilience, looking for climate change action in central Ohio. His album of activist songs raising awareness about the climate crisis entitled *Dance Floor at the Edge of Time,* has been performed in six states.

Between 1997 and 1999, his second wife Leslie and he adopted two children from Guatemala, Noël and Noah. Currently he is translating the poetry of Chilean poet Christian Formoso, publishing Formoso's masterpiece *The Most Beautiful Cemetery in Chile.* From August of 2021 to May of 2023, he helped guide immersions in Cadine Navarro's art installation, *It Sounds Like Love* at the Frank Museum of Otterbein University in Westerville, Ohio and at the Grange Insurance Audubon Center in Columbus, Ohio, an experience which led to this book.

About the Artist

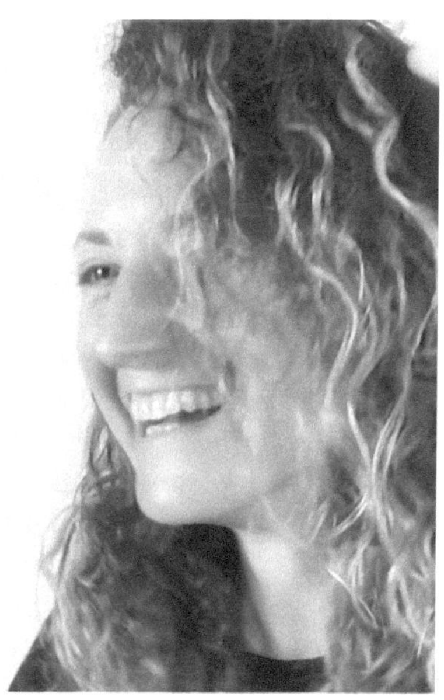

Cadine Navarro is a French-American artist currently living in Cambridge, Massachusetts, where she is working at MIT to further her research into the sounds of seeds. Her work has been shown extensively around the world, including the Wexner Center for the Arts, Venice Biennale, Contour Biennale, Art Brussels, and Deitch Studios New York. Though her father is French and her mother comes from Cleveland, Ohio, they moved to Japan just before she was born. She lived there for her first 17 years before a major earthquake destroyed their home and much of their city, sending her family into exile. She has since lived on three continents and in over 55 homes. Very much a land-based artist, Cadine Navarro's practice cross-pollinates the fields of art, science, design, and spirituality to create spaces of encounter and direct experience involving all the senses. More information can be found at: www.cadinenavarro.com.

Books by Bottom Dog Press

Harmony Series

Tiny Songs: Haiku & Meditations, by Terry Hermsen, 136 pgs., $16
Hope as a Construction, by David Adams, 182 pgs., $18
Baltic Amber in a Chest: Poems, by Clarissa Jakobsons, 104 pgs., $16
Choices: Three Novellas by Annabel Thomas, 176 pgs., $18
Pottery Town Blues, by Karen Kotrba, 128 pgs., $16
The Pears: Poems, by Larry Smith, 66 pgs, $15
Cycling Through Columbine, by JRW Case, 258 pgs., $18
Without a Plea, by Jeff Gundy, 96 pgs, $16
Taking a Walk in My Animal Hat, by Charlene Fix, 90 pgs, $16
Earnest Occupations, by Richard Hague, 200 pgs, $18
Pieces: A Composite Novel, by Mary Ann McGuigan, 250 pgs, $18
Crows in the Jukebox: Poems, by Mike James, 106 pgs, $16
Portrait of the Artist as a Bingo Worker: A Memoir, by Lori Jakiela, 216 pgs, $18
The Thick of Thin: A Memoir, by Larry Smith, 238 pgs, $18
Cold Air Return: A Novel, by Patrick Lawrence O'Keeffe, 390 pgs, $20
Flesh and Stones: A Memoir, by Jan Shoemaker, 176 pgs, $18
Waiting to Begin: A Memoir, by Patricia O'Donnell, 166 pgs, $18
And Waking: Poems, by Kevin Casey, 80 pgs, $16
Both Shoes Off: Poems, by Jeanne Bryner, 112 pgs, $16
Abandoned Homeland: Poems, by Jeff Gundy, 96 pgs, $16
Stolen Child: A Novel, by Suzanne Kelly, 338 pgs, $18

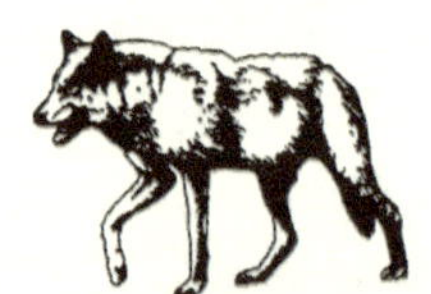

Bottom Dog Press, Inc.
P.O. Box 425 /Huron, Ohio 44839
http://smithdocs.net

Books by Bottom Dog Press

Harmony Series

The Canary: A Novel, by Michael Loyd Gray, 196 pgs, $18
On the Flyleaf: Poems, by Herbert Woodward Martin, 106 pgs, $16
The Harmonist at Nightfall: Poems of Indiana, by Shari Wagner, 114 pgs, $16
Painting Bridges: A Novel, by Patricia Averbach, 234 pgs, $18
Ariadne & Other Poems, by Ingrid Swanberg, 120 pgs, $16
The Search for the Reason Why: New and Selected Poems, by Tom Kryss, 192 pgs, $16
Kenneth Patchen: Rebel Poet in America, by Larry Smith, Revised 2nd Edition, 326 pgs, Cloth $28
Selected Correspondence of Kenneth Patchen, Edited with introduction by Allen Frost, Paper $18/ Cloth $28
Awash with Roses: Collected Love Poems of Kenneth Patchen, Eds. Laura Smith and Larry Smith with introduction by Larry Smith, 200 pgs, $16
Breathing the West: Great Basin Poems, by Liane Ellison Norman, 96 pgs, $16
Maggot: A Novel, by Robert Flanagan, 262 pgs, $18
American Poet: A Novel, by Jeff Vande Zande, 200 pgs, $18
The Way-Back Room: Memoir of a Detroit Childhood, by Mary Minock, 216 pgs, $18

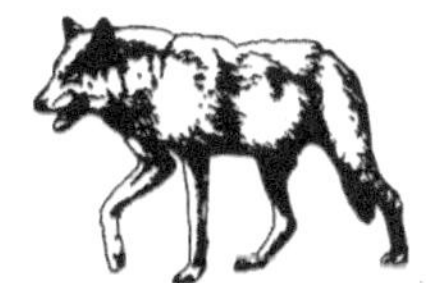

Bottom Dog Press, Inc.
P.O. Box 425 /Huron, Ohio 44839
http://smithdocs.net